W9-ADR-908

Make a Witch,
Make a Goblin

Make a Witch, Make a Goblin

A Book of Halloween Crafts

by Arnold Dobrin

Four Winds Press
New York

LIBRARY OF CONGRESS CATALOGING IN PUBLICATION DATA

Dobrin, Arnold.
Make a witch, make a goblin.

SUMMARY: Instructions for making costumes, party decorations, trick-or-treat bags, puppets, and party food, all on a Halloween theme.
1. Handicraft—Juvenile literature. 2. Cookery—Juvenile literature. 3. Halloween decorations—Juvenile literature. [1. Handicraft. 2. Cookery. 3. Halloween] I. Title.
TT160.D63 745.59'41 77–177
ISBN 0–590–07450–4

Published by Four Winds Press
A Division of Scholastic Magazines, Inc., New York, N.Y.

Printed in the United States of America
Library of Congress Catalog Card Number: 77–177
2 3 4 5 81 80 79 78

Contents

Introduction **2**

How to Use the Directions in This Book *6*

Costumes, Masks, and Other Disguises **8**

Basic Witch Dress Pattern *10*

One-Piece Basic Costume *14*

Pumpkin Costume *16*

Gathered Skirt Pattern *18*

Bat Costume *20*

Scarecrow Costume *22*

Big Trick-or-Treat Cat Costume *24*

Hats: Wizard Hat, Top Hat, Witch Hat *26*

Eyeglasses *29*

Long Witch's Nose *30*

Wizard or Clown Collar *32*

Black Cat Bow *33*

Crepe Paper Wig *34*

Yarn Wig *35*

Beard and Moustache *36*

More Moustaches and Other Disguises *38*

Papier-Mâché Masks *40*

Paper Bag Masks: Cat Mask, Funny Professor Mask, Wise Owl Mask, Wicked Goblin Mask, Silly Clown Mask *42*

Devil's Horns *45*

Paper Plate Masks *46*

Halloween Party Decorations—and Invitations, Place Cards and Favors 48
Witch Centerpiece *50*
Large Pumpkin Centerpiece *52*
Small Pumpkin Centerpiece *53*
Bat Mobile *54*
Paper Plate Skeleton *56*
Ghost Mobile *57*
Skull Noisemaker *58*
Pipe Cleaner Skeleton Mobile *59*
Black Cat Mobile *60*
Little Witch Mobile *62*
Jack-o'-Lantern Mobile *64*
Tin Can Noisemaker *66*
Witch and Pumpkin Party Invitations *68*
Party Place Cards *70*
Pompon Pets *72*
Paper Pumpkin Candy Cup *74*
Big Nose Paper Cup Witch *76*
Wise Owl Pin *78*
Black Cat Bookmark *79*
Scarecrows and Jack-o'-Lanterns and Trick-or-Treat Bags 80
Garden Scarecrow *82*
Porch Scarecrow *84*
Jack-o'-Lanterns *85*
Trick-or-Treat Bags *86*
Halloween Puppet Theater 88
Easy Finger Puppets *90*

Cat Sock Puppets *91*
Hand Puppets: Witch, Cat, Ghost, Goblins *92*
Wraparound Finger Puppets:
Ghost, Witch, Monster *94*
Witch and Ghost String Puppets *96*
Puppet Stage *98*
Halloween Party Food 100
The Wonderful Pumpkin *102*
Crispy Pumpkin Pie Crust *104*
Spicy Pumpkin Pie Filling *105*
Crunchy Pumpkin Seeds *106*
Sweet Pumpkin Bread *107*
Pumpkin Cake *108*
Jack-o'-Lantern Fruit Cup *109*
Halloween Carrot Doughnuts *110*
Witch's Brew and Easy Witch's Brew *112*
Halloween Candied Apples *113*
Halloween Carrot Cake *114*
Halloween Carrot-Fruit Dessert *115*
Gingerbread Witches, Ghosts, and Pumpkins *116*
Carrot Salad *117*
Basic Creamy Frosting *118*
How to Make a Decorating Tube for Frosting *119*
Cookie Decorating Tips *120*

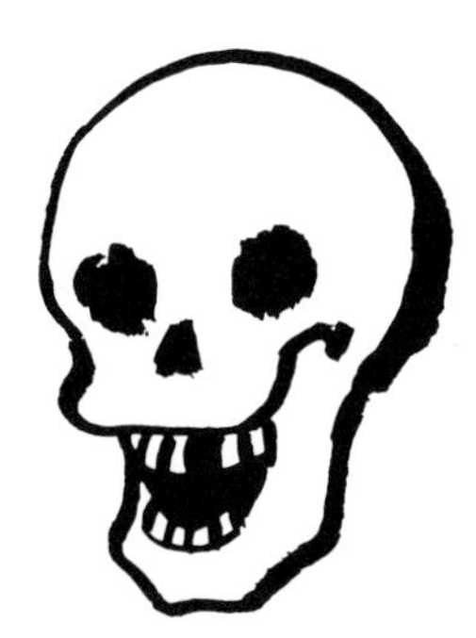

Make a Witch, Make a Goblin

Introduction

Witches riding broomsticks through the cold night air! Ghosts and goblins dancing around graveyard tombstones! Black cats dashing around with their fur standing straight up! This is Halloween, a time of fun, excitement, good times—and just a little fear.

Thousands of years ago men and women who lived in western Europe also celebrated Halloween but they called it by a different name. These people were the Druids and their celebration was called Samhain.

Samhain marked the beginning of winter—a time of snow, ice, great cold and long dark nights. On the Celtic calendar, which was used by the Druids, October 31 was the last day of the year. The Druids knew that after this date many of them would die during the long, cold winter ahead. They believed, too, that evil spirits, witches and ghosts came forth on this night to choose those who would die.

Hoping to turn away these evil and frightening creatures, the Druids built great bonfires. Their priests recited special prayers. Masks were worn so that the evil spirits would not be able to recognize any of the living. In this way the Druids hoped to turn away death. They hoped to conquer their fear of the long, cruel winter which lay ahead.

As Christianity developed it often used pagan rites—such as those of the Druids—as a part of the Christian religion. But the Christian priests changed the names of

the pagan festivals. The feast of Samhain became All Hallows or All Saint's Eve. Although the name was changed, the basic idea of the holiday remained the same.

When the first settlers came to America they brought their love of All Hallows Eve with them. But eventually the name was changed again—this time to Halloween. Some of the ways it was celebrated were also changed. The settlers had never used pumpkins before because pumpkins do not grow in Europe. Soon, however, they realized that the huge vegetables make wonderful grinning jack-o'-lanterns.

Since that distant time the jack-o'-lanterns, as well as all of the other details of the Halloween celebration, have contributed to one of the best-loved holidays in America. For children, especially, it is one of the most exciting times of the year.

This book was written to help you enjoy it more. For Halloween means changing who you are. It means dressing up to become a witch or ghost, a pirate or black cat. It means eating special delicious food and having fun of many kinds. Halloween means *making* things.

The craft projects described in this book make use of everyday materials which many people have in their homes. If you *don't* find them in your home you will discover that they are not very expensive to buy. Many stores have special counters where odd ends of fabric are sold cheaply. Construction paper is available in art supply stores and

most five-and-ten-cent stores. Craft stores have a wider range of material and can be fun to browse in before you begin to make your Halloween crafts.

Both craft and art stores have a great many interesting papers. Some are rough, others are coarse, shiny or smooth. Most come in a great many beautiful colors. Ordinary construction paper can be used for most of the crafts in this book, but you should feel free to try other papers.

If you feel that the paper you want costs too much, buy as little as possible and experiment first with newspapers. After you are sure you have the experiment right, go ahead and make it with the construction and other papers.

When cardboard paper is needed, it can be cut from boxes which are probably in your own home. If you can't find any, go to your local stores and ask for boxes that are going to be thrown away. The clerks will probably be glad to give them to you.

Brown paper bags which come from the grocery store are valuable and can be used in several ways. Save these and keep them in good condition. Plastic containers (such as gallon bleach containers) can be cut and decorated to make excellent masks. Ask your mother or father to save these for you so that you will have enough when Halloween time comes.

Don't be content to use only the materials listed in this book. If you keep your eyes open you will probably find many things you can use for your Halloween crafts.

Explore your attic. Explore your basement. Search for interesting things such as feathers, buttons or old clothes. Many kinds of old clothes will make funny scarecrows. Old hats are especially useful in Halloween crafts. Finding these things is almost as much fun as making the costumes, masks and other things you will need for Halloween. There's no doubt about it—Halloween is *fun*.

How to Use the Directions in This Book

Basic Equipment

At the beginning of the directions for each project is a list of the materials that will be needed. However, the *tools* needed are *not* listed. They are ordinary tools—such as scissors and needles—that are found in every house. It is up to you to collect these items before you begin work on the Halloween crafts projects.

How to Trace

Many patterns are included in the directions for the crafts projects. There are two ways to make use of these.

One is to take a piece of tracing paper and trace over the pattern in the book. You can then cut around the traced drawing and lay it flat on the paper or fabric you are going to use. Pencil *around* the traced drawing and cut out the paper or fabric shape.

The second way to transfer a tracing is to use the tracing paper as in the first example. But then, instead of cutting around it, lay it on top of a piece of carbon paper which has been placed on top of the paper you are going to use. Make sure the carbon side is facing this paper. Trace the lines firmly over the traced drawing you have already made. The pressure will reproduce the lines on the paper beneath the carbon.

Types of Paper

The basic material for most of the craftwork in this book is paper. Construction paper, cover stock, oak tag or poster board can be used for almost all of the crafts projects, so use whichever is available. Sometimes these papers are called by different names in certain areas so it is a good idea to visit your local art store and see what papers are available and learn what they are called.

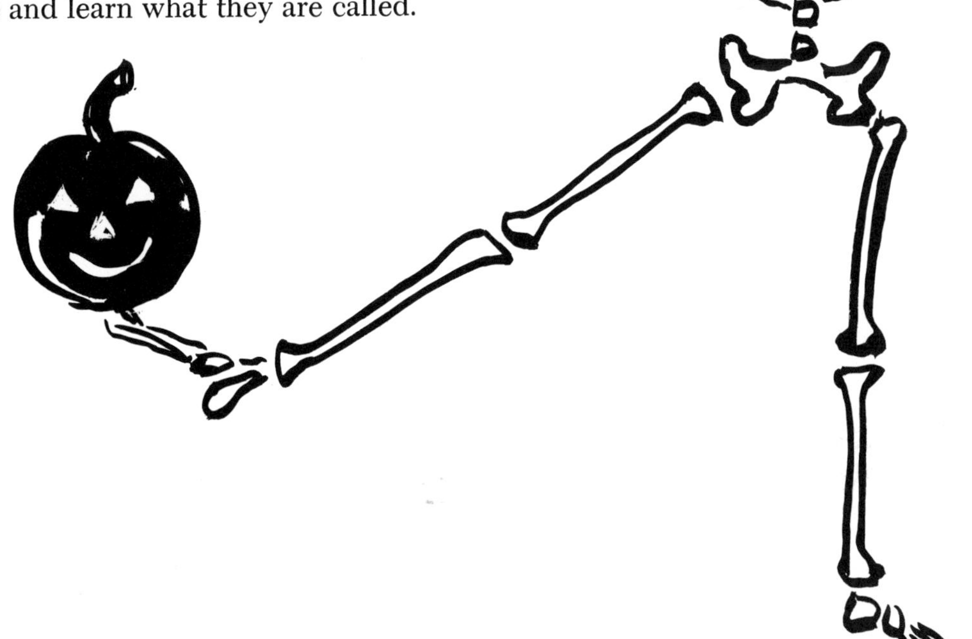

Costumes, Masks,

and Other Disguises

Basic Witch Dress Pattern

Materials:

45″-wide fabric
  2 yds. for 3′ child
  3 yds. for 4′ child
Chalk
Thread

Method:

1. First you must measure the person who is going to wear the costume. If you are making it for yourself, ask one of your parents or a friend to measure you. This is what you do:
   a. Sleeves: measure from the tips of the fingers of your extended arm to the center back of the neck. Add 2″ for the hem.
   b. Body: measure your height from your collar bone to the floor. Add 2″ for the hem.
   c. Width: to half your hip measurement, add 5″.
2. Using these measurements, make a pattern for the dress as shown in the diagram at the top of the page. Make the sleeve 16″ wide.
3. Fold the material in half with the selvages together. Selvage edges are the edges of the material that are not cut, but are smoothly finished off. The selvage edges are shown in the diagram by the ragged lines.
4. Draw the pattern onto the material as you see it in the bottom diagram. Cut it out. The measurements you have taken are for *half* the front or *half* the back of the

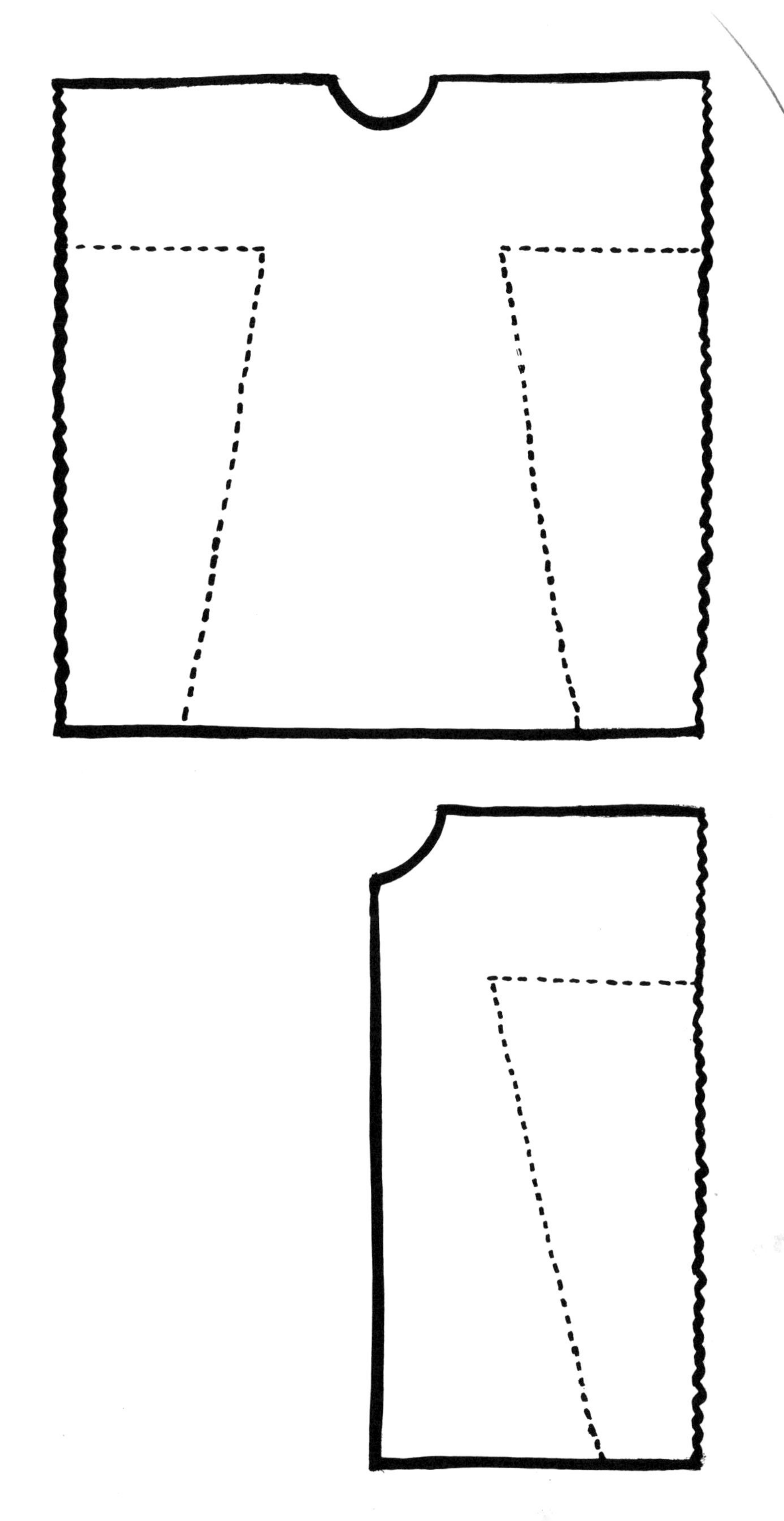

dress. When measured from the fold and cut out, the piece of material you have is the *entire* front or back of the dress.

5. Repeat steps 3 and 4 to get the other side of your dress.
6. Cut a small half circle 4″ across out of the top center of material for the neck opening.
7. Cut a 4″ slit from the circle down the back.
8. Place the two pieces of material together with the right sides facing each other and sew the shoulder, arm, and side seams.
9. Turn under 2″ of material on each sleeve and on the bottom of the dress for the hems. Sew the hems.
10. Turn under about ½″ of material on the neck edge and along the slit and sew for a smooth finish. Sew a snap to close the slit at the neck edge.
11. A belt may be made from the same material to gather your dress at the waist.

One-Piece Basic Costume

(Suitable for animal bodies and skeletons)

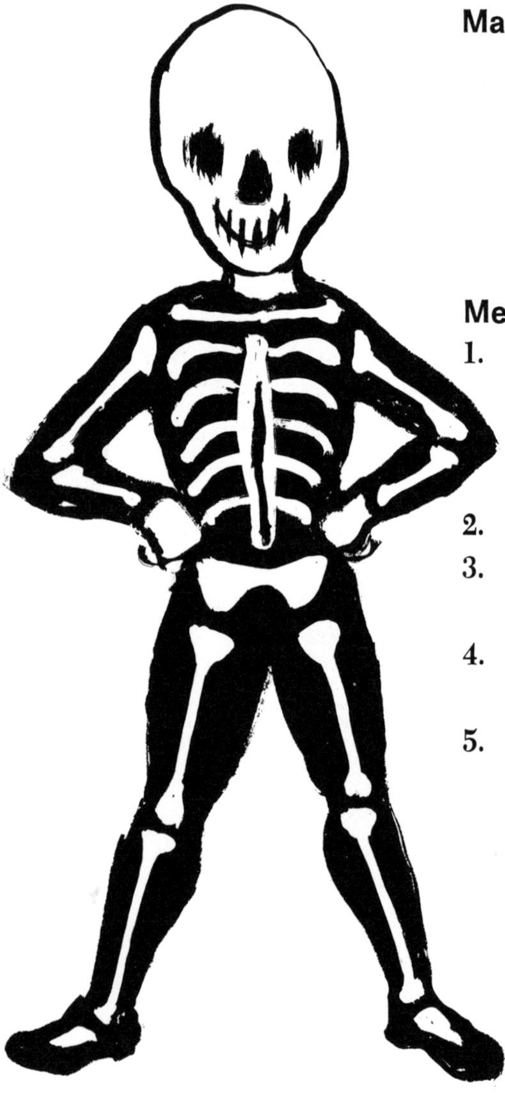

Materials:

Fabric—45″ wide
  2 yds. for 3′ child
  3 yds. for 4′ child
Chalk
Thread

Method:

1. Fold the material in half (right sides facing each other) and lay it on the floor. Lie down upon the fabric with your shoulders along the fold. Your arms should be outstretched.
2. Ask a friend to trace around your body.
3. Before cutting out the pattern, add 6″ to the traced edge to allow for the body width and seam allowance.
4. Also add 4″ to the ends of the arm and leg openings for ease.
5. Cut along the seam line. Also, around the middle of the fold, cut a small circle 4″ in diameter. The diameter is the width of a circle across its center, the widest part. To draw a circle with a 4″ diameter, tie a piece of string to a pencil. Then, measuring the string from the pencil, cut the string at the point that is half the diameter of the circle you are drawing. For a circle with a 4″ diameter, cut the string 2″ from the pencil. Hold the

end of the string in the middle of the material (or whatever you are drawing the circle on) with your finger. Keep the string tight while you draw the pencil in a circle around your finger. In this way you can draw any size circle you want.

6. Cut a 4″ slit for the neck opening.
7. With the right sides together, sew along the seam lines.
8. Sew a snap to close the slit at the neck edge.
9. Sleeve, neck, and leg openings may be hemmed, if you like.

TIGER

1. Use yellow or orange material.
2. After you've finished sewing, paint black stripes onto the material.
3. Sew a tube out of a piece of material approximately 24″ long and 3″ wide. Stuff it with newspaper and sew it to the back of the costume for a tail.

SKELETON

1. Use black material.
2. After you've finished sewing, paint bones on the material with white paint.

BLACK CAT

1. Use black material and add the mask described on page 42. You may want to add the black cat bow described on page 33.

Pumpkin Costume

Materials:

One package of 1-ply orange crepe paper
Heavy string and a large needle
Black construction paper
Black fabric
Glue

Method:

1. Using the entire package, glue the ends of all the sheets of crepe paper together to form one big circular piece.
2. With heavy thread, gather loosely both the top and bottom edges of the circle of paper. Leave the ends of the thread hanging loose for now.
3. Wear dark pants. Ask a friend to help you place the crepe paper around yourself, from shoulders to hips. Gather the top tightly and knot the threads together.
4. Cut holes in the sides for your arms.
5. Stuff the "pumpkin" with newspapers and then gather the bottom tightly. Knot the threads.
6. Cut eyes, a nose and a mouth out of black construction paper and glue them in place on the crepe paper.
7. Sew a black hood (in the shape of a pillow case) to fit your head, and cut holes for the eyes, nose, and mouth. Or you can use a plain black mask instead.

Gathered Skirt Pattern

Materials:

Fabric

36″ material—about 1½ yd. for each skirt

45″ material—about 1 yd. for each skirt

There will be some material left over if you make a short skirt.

Chalk

Elastic

Thread

Method:

1. Ask someone to measure you from the waist to the desired length for your skirt. Add 3″ for an elastic casing at the top and 2″ for the hem at the bottom.
2. Measure your hips, and then double that measurement for the width.
3. Using these measurements, cut out a rectangular piece of material.
4. With the right sides together, sew up the back seam.
5. Turn the fabric over 3″ at the top to the wrong side and sew the fabric down, forming a casing for the elastic. Leave a small opening along the seam line.
6. Measure and cut a piece of elastic the same size as your waist, plus 2″ for the overlapping.
7. Thread the elastic through the hole in the casing. As you thread the elastic through, the skirt will automatically gather at the waist to fit you. Overlap the ends of the elastic and sew them together.
8. Turn up 2″ at the bottom of the skirt for a hem and sew it in place.

Bat Costume

Materials:

Black fabric, 1 yd. of 36″-wide material
Thread
Snaps
Black felt, 1 small rectangle, 9″ x 12″
White chalk

Method:

1. Outstretch your arms and measure across your shoulders from fingertip to fingertip. Ask a friend or adult to help you measure.
2. Cut a piece of black fabric as wide as that measurement and 36″ long. If you are small, adjust the length to suit your size.
3. In the middle of the top edge cut out an oval (with an opening along the top edge) that is large enough to fit around your neck. Sew on a snap.
4. Using white chalk, draw a scalloped edge that looks like the wing shape of a bat. Cut the fabric along the chalk line to form your bat wings.
5. Sew a small loop of material at each top corner to fit over your index finger. This will enable you to raise your arms and extend the bat wings.
6. Using the same black fabric, make a hood shaped like a pillow case, but with two rounded corners.
7. Draw facial features on the hood with white chalk and cut them out.

8. Cut two triangles out of the felt for ears. Sew these onto the top of the hood.
9. Wear a black shirt and pants to complete your costume.

Scarecrow Costume

Materials:

Old pants and jacket
Brown paper bags
Straw (optional). In the autumn one can gather the stalks of sturdy weeds and dry them. Old brooms, or new ones, are also sources for the material. And straw types of material can be had at craft stores.
Crayons or magic markers
Glue
String or rope

Method:

1. For the scarecrow's head, crumple a large brown paper bag until it is soft. Cut out the eyes and a nose, and draw on a mouth.
2. Glue pieces of straw or strips of brown paper to the top and sides of the bag for hair. Put the bag on your head and tie it loosely around your neck with string.
3. Put on old clothes.
4. Stuff straw or strips of brown paper into your sleeves and pants legs so that the straw or paper will extend over your hands and feet.
5. Tie string around your wrists and ankles so the straw or paper will not fall out.
6. A floppy hat and broom can be used to complete the costume.

Big Trick-or-Treat Cat Costume

Materials:

Black leotard
Black felt
Big paper bag or shopping bag
Black felt-tip pen
Paint (optional)
One wire coat hanger, unwound and straightened
Heavy black thread

Method:

1. Put on the black leotard.
2. Use the black felt to make a black head covering shaped like a pillow case.
3. Cover the wire by twisting and glueing 1″ strips of black felt around the wire. Bend one end of the wire into a small loop and sew this onto the leotard with heavy thread to form the cat's tail.
4. Cut the bottom out of the bag.
5. Write "trick or treat" on each side of the bag with the felt-tip pen.
6. Cut a 4″-wide hole out of each of the smaller side panels of the bag, about 4″ down from the top.
7. Put the bag on over your body with your arms out the holes at the sides.
8. Add the cat mask described in the section on masks.

TRICK
OR
TREAT

Hats

WIZARD HAT

Materials:

White and colored construction papers (shiny colored papers are especially good for decorating this hat). Use poster board or cover stock for a sturdier hat

Colored paper or yarn pompon (instructions on page 72)

Glue or staples

Method:

1. Using a piece of white construction paper 12″ x 18″, form a cone shape.
2. Hold the cone in place and try it on for size. Adjust it if it is not right.
3. Glue or staple the cone together.
4. Following the designs in this book, cut different shapes out of the colored paper. You can make stars, a moon, or whatever looks best.
5. Paste the shapes on the hat. Paste on the pompon.

TOP HAT

Materials:

Black and colored construction paper
Glue or staples

METHOD:

1. Using the black construction paper, make a tube 8″ to 10″ tall and wide enough to fit your head. If one sheet isn't large enough, glue or tape two pieces together.
2. Attach the two sides of the paper with glue or staples.
3. Take the tube you have just made, stand it on end, and trace a circle on black paper by drawing around the outside of the tube.
4. Cut out the circle and attach it to one end of the tube with tape from the *inside* of the hat.
5. Trace another circle the same size as the tube opening, as you did before. In several spots, measure 2″ from the outside of this circle and place pencil dots at these spots. Connect these dots with a pencil to form another circle. This 2″ band is the brim of the hat. Cut this out of the paper and then cut away the center circle of paper. Using black tape, attach the brim to the hat from the inside of the hat.
6. Cut a bright strip of colored paper about 1″ wide and glue it on for a hat band.

WITCH HAT

Materials:

1 sheet of black construction paper
1 sheet of silver paper
1 piece of red or orange crepe paper
4 metal paper fasteners
Glue

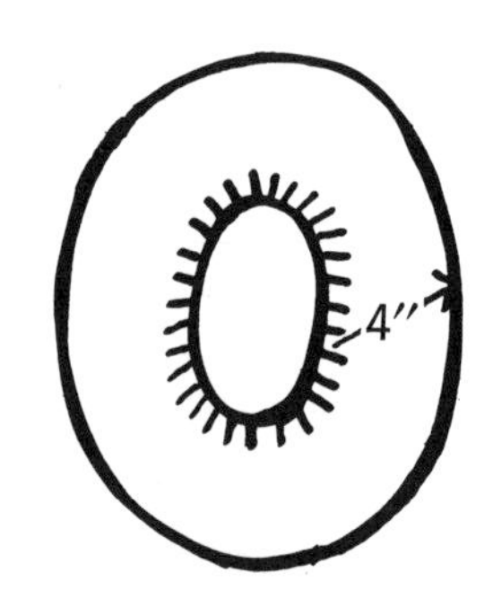

Method:

1. Using the appropriate size diameter as given below, draw a circle on the construction paper. Follow the directions for making a circle given on page 14.
   7″ diameter for small children—4 yrs. and under
   7½″ diameter for older children—5 to 10 yrs.
   8″ diameter for teenage and adult.
2. Draw another circle 4″ from the outside of the circle you have just drawn. Cut around this outer circle and then cut away the inner circle. This makes the brim.
3. Using the sizes in the diagram, cut the crown from the same paper.
4. Overlap the sides of the crown to form a conical shape and fasten with paper fasteners.
5. Tape the brim to the crown from the inside.
6. Cut a band of red or orange crepe paper and glue it around the crown.
7. Cut a buckle out of the silver paper and glue it onto the band.

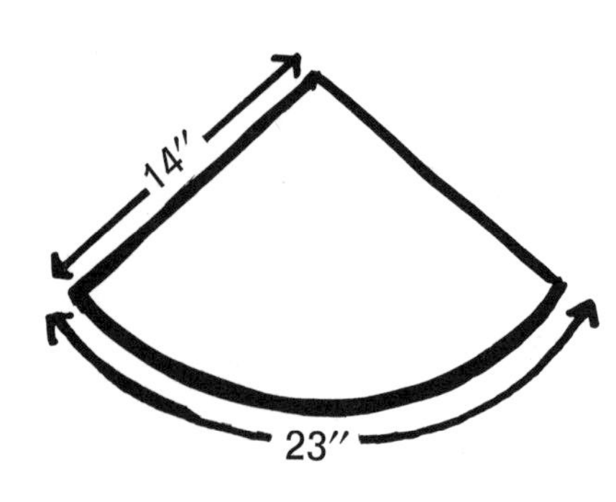

Eyeglasses

Materials:

8″-long pipe cleaners. (The colored chenille type are especially good for this disguise.)

Clear adhesive tape

Method:

1. Bend two of the pipe cleaners into two rings about 2″ across. Twist the ends so that each circle is secure.
2. Cut one 3″ piece of pipe cleaner. Twist 1″ of each end onto the inside of each ring. This is the nose bridge, which should be about 1″ wide.
3. For the parts that fit over your ears, twist two 8″ stems onto the outside of each ring. Curve the ends so that they will fit around your ears.

NOTE: The glasses may be a little wobbly on your head. Use bobby pins to hold them on if necessary.

Long Witch's Nose

Materials:

White or pink construction paper
String
White, red, and yellow poster paint (optional)
Brown poster paint (optional)
Stapler or rubber cement
Notebook ring reinforcements

Method:

1. If you want a white nose go directly to step 2. If you want a flesh-colored nose, mix your red, white and yellow paint to get a flesh color. Start with a little white paint and add a few dabs of red and yellow. Mix the colors thoroughly, and then add more red or yellow to get just the shade you want. Or, if the color is too strong, add a little more white paint to lighten the color. Or you may want a brown nose. Paint the white paper with whatever color you have chosen. Allow it to dry thoroughly.

2. Draw a circle with a diameter of 6″ on the paper, following directions on page 14. Cut the circle in half. You will need only one half for this project.
3. Form a cone from the half circle by joining together the two ends of the straight side.
4. Glue or staple these two ends together.
5. Make two holes on either side of the cone.
6. Put a notebook reinforcement on the inside of both holes.
7. Cut 2 pieces of string about 23″ long and attach the ends to the holes of the cone. Place the cone over your own nose and tie the strings around your head to keep the nose in place.

(These directions are for a 3″ long nose. For a longer nose, use a larger circle cut in half.)

Wizard or Clown Collar

Materials:

Newspapers
Heavy thread
Spray paint (optional)

Method:

1. Cut the newspapers into 8″ squares. Approximately 100 pieces are needed. You can cut several squares at once by stacking several sheets of newspaper on top of each other and then cutting.
2. Put 2 squares on top of each other and fold them into quarters. Do this with all the rest of the squares.
3. Knot the thread and sew through the closed corner formed by the folded edges of the squares.
4. Sew through all the rest of the folded pieces, and when the collar is full enough, tie it around your neck.
5. To make a more colorful collar you can use comics or you can paint the paper any color you choose.

Black Cat Bow

You can use this bow with either the black cat version of the one-piece basic costume, page 15, or the big trick-or-treat cat costume, page 24.

Materials:

1¾ yards of ribbon 3″ to 5″ wide. (Velvet, grosgrain, taffeta and satin make the best bows.) Both black and orange look very good with any cat costume.

Method:

This bow is tied just as you would tie your shoelaces. If you don't know how to do this, ask someone to help you. Adjust your bow so there are no wrinkles.

Crepe Paper Wig

Materials:

Black crepe paper
Glue

Method:

1. Decide on the length of your wig by measuring down from the center of your head to however long you want the hair to be.
2. Cut two pieces of black crepe paper 6″ wide and the same length as you decided the hair should be.
3. Glue the two pieces together along the 6″ side and cut each side into strips for strands of hair. Cut only to within 2″ of the center seam on each side. When following the rest of the directions, think of this glued seam as the part down the middle of your head.
4. Cut another piece 6″ wide and half as long as the other pieces. Leaving the top 2″ solid, cut this piece into strands.
5. Glue this piece underneath the back section of the wig.
6. Cut a piece of paper 3″ x 3″. Cut this into strips to form bangs and glue it to the front of the wig from underneath.
7. If you want more hair on your wig, add more layers of cut crepe paper.

Yarn Wig

Materials:

Yarn (4 oz. of knitting worsted, whatever color you wish your hair to be)
Cloth (4″ x 5″)
A piece of cardboard, wood, or a large book

Method:

1. Decide on the length of your wig by measuring from the center of your head to the desired length.
2. Find a book, a board or a piece of cardboard that is close to the length you want. Wrap the yarn around it 250 times.
3. Cut through one end of the wrapped yarn.
4. Cut 50 pieces of yarn 4″ long for bangs.
5. Cut a rectangle of cloth 4″ x 5″.
6. Sew the yarn for the bangs across one 4″ end of the cloth. Sew on a sewing machine or by hand. If you sew by hand, use very small stitches and sew across the yarn 3 times to make sure you secure all the pieces.
7. Take out 50 pieces of the long yarn. Fold them in half and sew the folded edges to the other 4″ end.
8. Place the rest of the cut yarn across the piece of material, from one 5″ end to the other, and sew it down the middle, making certain that the other stitching is covered. This seam will resemble the part in your own hair.
9. Cut the corners of the fabric if they are visible under the bangs.
10. Trim the yarn if necessary.

Beard and Moustache

Materials:

Yellow, brown, or black construction paper, depending on the color of beard and moustache you want
String
Masking tape
Brown felt-tip pen (if you are making a yellow beard)
Notebook ring reinforcements
Yellow or black yarn (optional)
Tissue paper or tracing paper

Method:

1. Cut the construction paper to a rectangle 8″ or 10½″ long. Fold it in half.
2. Trace the pattern on the next page onto a piece of tissue paper and then transfer it to the construction paper, using the tracing directions given on pages 6-7.
3. Cut out the pattern.
4. Draw hair on the "beard" with a pen or chalk, or glue yarn to it to look like hair.
5. Make a hole in each side of the beard. Glue a reinforcement around the hole.
6. Cut two pieces of string about 17″ long. Attach one to each hole, and then tie the ends behind your head to secure the beard.

NOTE: To make a moustache without the beard, use only the bottom part of the pattern on the next page. This can be attached to your face with tape.

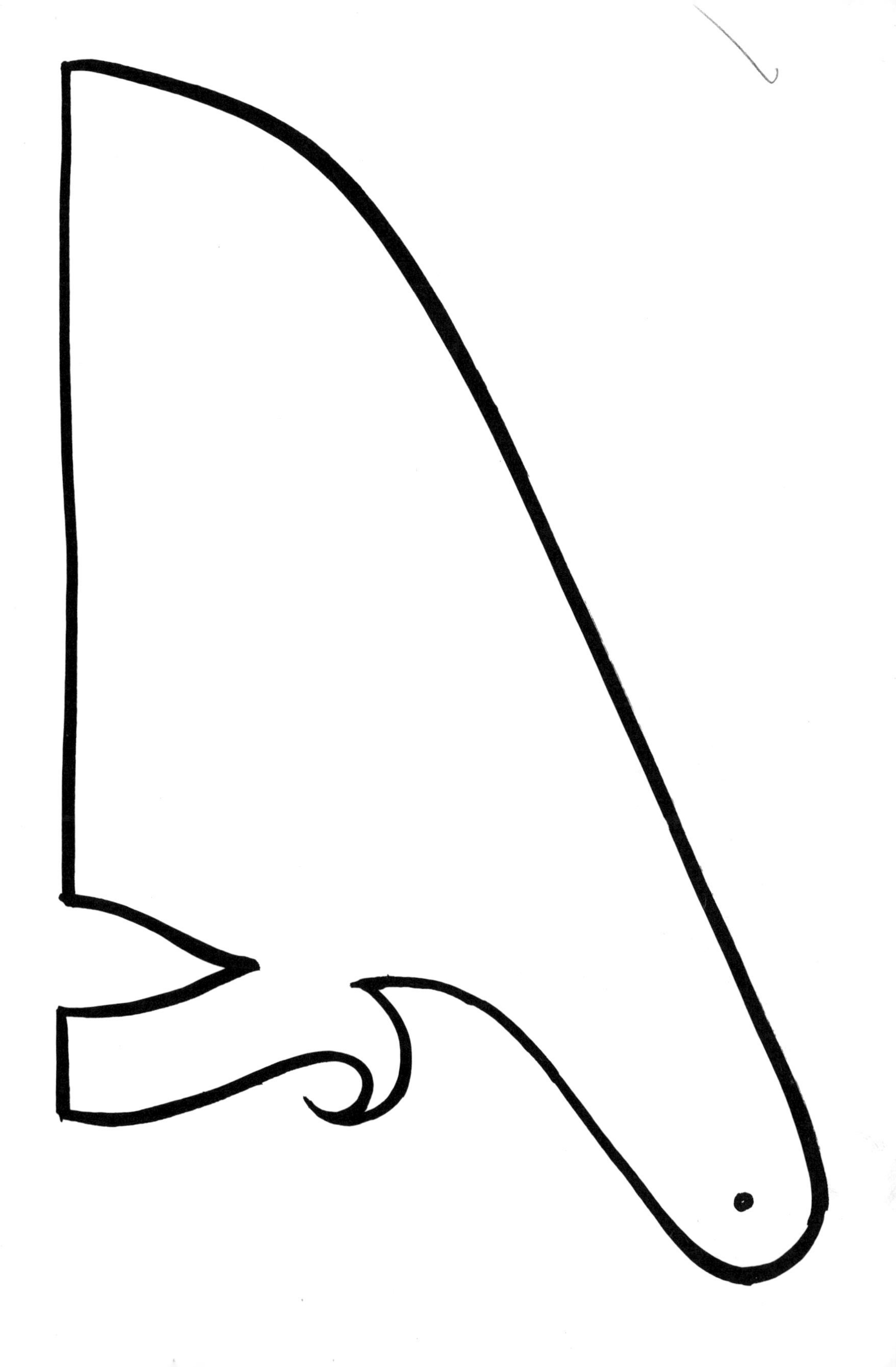

More Moustaches and Other Disguises

Materials:

Colored construction paper
Colored ribbon or string for eye patch
Tape
Glue

Methods:

1. Cut out the disguises following the patterns on the next page. Use whatever color construction paper you like.
2. Use little pieces of tape on the tabs of the eyebrow and nose to hold them in place. (The moustaches will remain in place if you fit the two little pieces at the top of each into your nostrils.)
3. Glue the upper part of the teeth behind the bottom of whichever moustache you like.

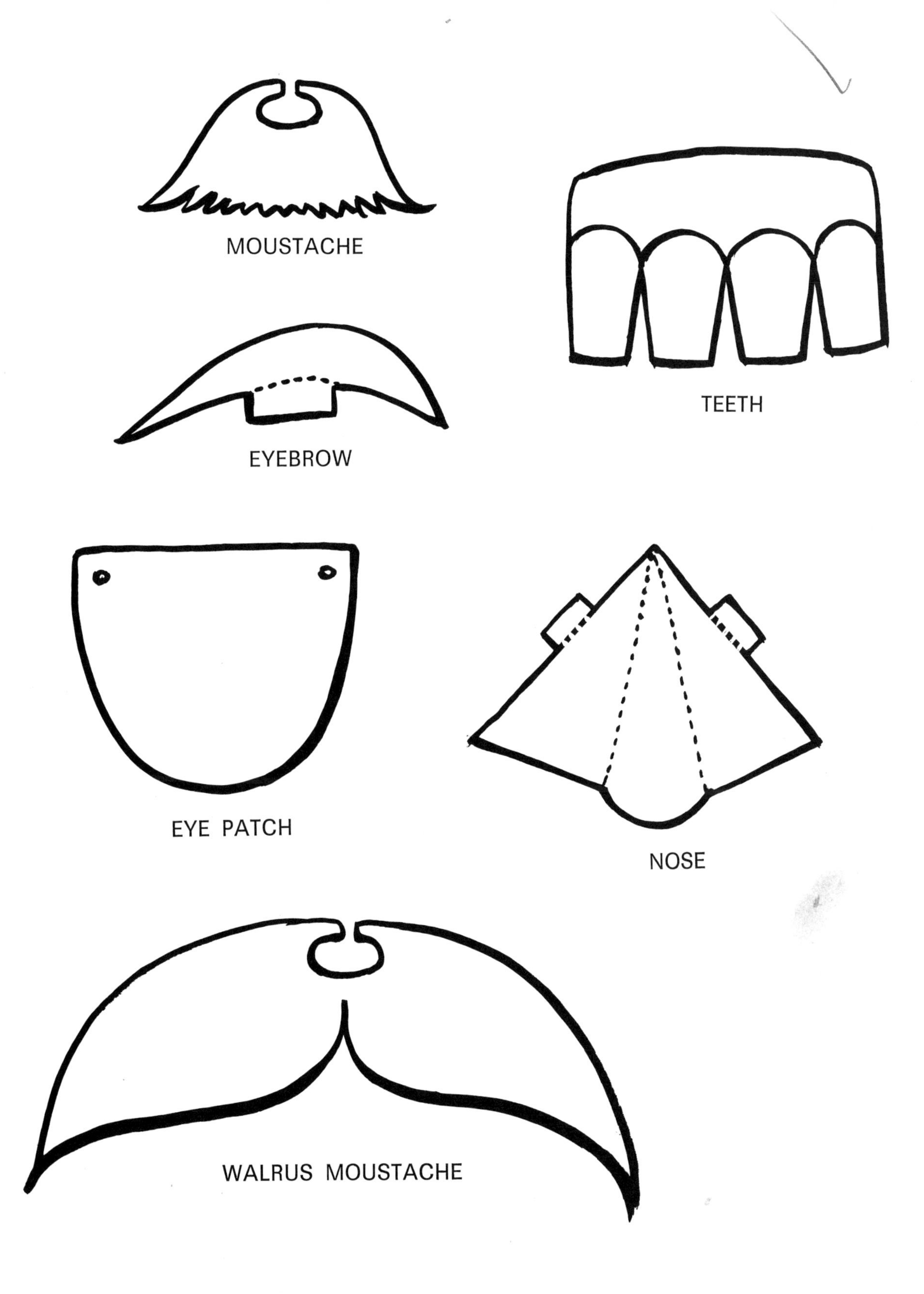
MOUSTACHE
TEETH
EYEBROW
EYE PATCH
NOSE
WALRUS MOUSTACHE

Papier-Mâché Masks

Materials:

Heavy-duty aluminum foil

Wheat paste, which can be bought in the paint department of discount stores. Also known as wallpaper paste.

Newspapers

Container for mixing paste

Poster paints of whatever colors you need for the character you're making

String

Method:

1. Using a double thickness of heavy-duty aluminum foil, make a mold of your face. Do this by pressing the foil over your whole face, making sure that it goes under your chin and around to your ears. When you have the outline of your whole face in the foil, carefully remove the foil and set it aside.
2. Tear the newspaper into 2″-wide strips.
3. In a bowl mix the wheat paste with water until it is smooth and has the consistency of thick mud.
4. Wet both sides of the newspaper strips with the paste and lay them over the foil face, being careful not to press too hard. Overlap each strip for strength.
5. Cover the foil twice, alternating the direction of the paper strips.
6. Place the mask somewhere to dry. It will take about one week to dry.

7. Remove the aluminum foil from the mask and trim the edges of the mask with scissors.
8. Cut out the eyes, a nose and a mouth.
9. Dip pieces of newspaper into the paste and squeeze them into shapes for the nose and eyebrows. Place these on the mask, and hold them in place by covering the shapes with another layer of newspaper strips dipped in paste.
10. Using the poster paints, paint the mask and features to resemble the character you are making.
11. Punch a small hole on each side of the mask. Tie a string through each hole long enough to reach around your head and tie in back.

Paper Bag Masks

Materials:

Brown paper bags from the grocery store
Glue
Poster paint or crayons
Felt-tip pens (wide tip size)
Construction paper in different colors
Straw
Yarn in different colors

Basic Method:

1. Trim the open end of the bag so that it fits comfortably over your head and rests on your shoulders.
2. Place the bag over your head and mark places for your eyes.
3. Draw the eyes and cut them out.
4. Follow the special directions for the type of mask you want to make.

CAT MASK

1. Paint the bag black or white. Set it aside to dry.
2. On a separate piece of black or white construction paper, draw a cat's face. Cut the face out and paste it to the bag.
3. Make cat ears and paste one to each side of the bag.
4. Glue on some straw for whiskers.
5. Tie a big pussy-cat bow around your neck.

FUNNY PROFESSOR MASK

1. The professor's ears can be cut from another paper and added on. Use the pattern to the right. Cut out two ears, fold along the dotted line, and glue or tape the small folded flap to the side of the mask.
2. Draw the professor's face on the mask.
3. Draw the professor's glasses and moustache on a separate piece of black construction paper and cut them out.
4. Glue these onto the mask.
5. Glue yarn on the top of the bag for the professor's hair.

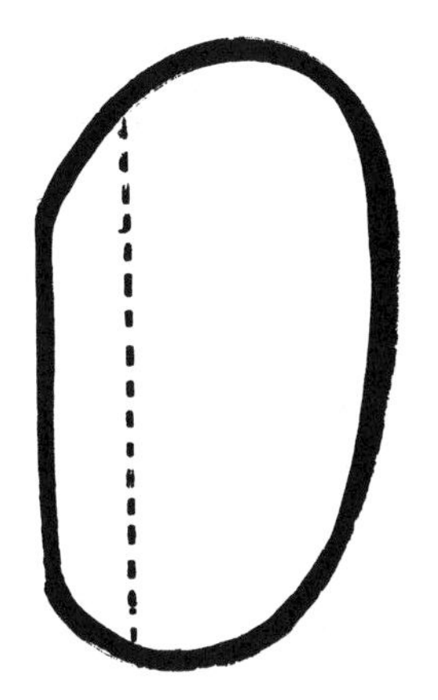

WISE OWL MASK

1. Cut the bottom of the paper bag as shown in the drawing to the left.
2. Draw round circles for the owl's eyes.
3. With white chalk, draw a forehead and a beak on a piece of black construction paper. Cut them out and paste them onto the paper bag.
4. Fold the bottom point out for a beak.

WICKED GOBLIN MASK

1. Draw the face, using the drawing on the left as a guide.
2. Make ears from the side of the paper bag.
3. Glue or staple white or black yarn onto the top of the bag for the goblin's hair.

SILLY CLOWN MASK

1. Draw the face, using the drawing on the left as a guide.
2. Draw ears and cut them out.
3. Make a clown hat, using the directions for a wizard hat on page 26.
4. Paste colored designs on the hat and top with a ball of yarn.

Devil's Horns

Materials:

Orange or black construction paper
Glue
Felt-tip pens
Wax

Method:

1. Cut a 1″-wide strip of paper long enough to fit around your head. Glue the ends together to form a circle.
2. Cut two triangles 8″ x 8″ x 11½″.
3. Glue together the two ends of the longest side of each triangle to form two cone shapes.
4. Put a little glue on the inside of the bottom edge of the cones, flatten the cones out, and glue the bottom edges together.
5. Glue the horns (cones) to the headband.
6. You can then decorate the horns with felt-tip pens.

Paper Plate Masks

Materials:

Newspapers
White paste
Poster paints
Paper plates (9-inch size)
Other materials you may want to use on these masks:
- Construction paper
- Fabric
- Felt
- Yarn
- Crepe paper
- Glitter

Method:

1. Make a pattern of your own face by doing the following, shown in the diagrams on the next page: Fold an 8-inch square of paper in half. Place the fold lengthwise down the center of your face. Mark the position of your eyes, nose and mouth.
2. Open the paper and draw the eyes, nose and mouth more carefully. Cut out the holes.
3. Transfer this pattern to the paper plate.
4. Cut the nose, eyes and mouth out of the paper plate.
5. Crumple a wad of damp newspaper for the nose.
6. Fasten it to the mask with strips of dry newspaper that are held down with glue. (You can also make eyebrows this way.)

7. When the mask is completely dry, paint all of the features with colored paint.
8. Attach colored yarn for the hair. (optional)

Halloween Party Invitations,

Decorations and Place Cards, and Favors

Witch Centerpiece

Materials:

Plastic detergent bottle
Styrofoam ball ($2\frac{1}{2}''$)
Black crepe paper
Black and orange construction paper
Small piece of white cardboard (or cover stock)
Glue and masking tape
2 pipe cleaners

Method:

1. Push the styrofoam ball onto the neck of the bottle.
2. Twist 2 pipe cleaners together for arms. Glue or tape them to the back of the bottle at shoulder level.
3. From the cardboard cut 2 hands and tape them to the ends of the pipe cleaner.
4. Cut a dress out of black crepe paper, using the directions for the basic pattern on pages 10 to 12. Make this dress small enough to fit the bottle you are using. Cut a small hole and a slit for the neckline. You won't need a snap for this dress.
5. With the right sides of the paper facing each other, tape or glue the side and arm seams together. Turn the dress right side out and place it on the bottle.
6. Using a thin piece of orange crepe or construction paper for a belt, tie the dress at the waist.
7. Cut the eyes, nose and mouth out of black construction paper and glue them to the styrofoam ball.
8. To make a hat, cut a circle 4″ in diameter out of black paper. Cut a slit straight from the edge to the center of the circle. Overlap the edges of this slit until the cone

fits the ball (head), and then glue or tape the edges together. Make a brim by tracing the open end of the hat and then adding another circle 2″ from that. Cut out this large circle and then cut out the center circle. This forms the brim. Tape the brim to the hat.

9. Draw a broom twice on the cardboard and cut out both pieces. Glue them together so the broom doesn't bend. Attach the broom with glue or tape to the witch's hand.
10. Make hair out of yarn, string or crepe paper and glue it onto the ball. Add the hat.

Large Pumpkin Centerpiece

Materials:

Orange crepe paper
Newspapers
Thread
Tape
Glue
Black, green, orange, red, and yellow construction paper

Method:

1. Cut a square piece of crepe paper 24″ x 24″ or larger. If the paper is not wide enough, glue or tape two pieces together.
2. Using needle and thread, sew a long running stitch around all the edges of the square.
3. Gather it partially and stuff it with small sections of crumpled newspaper.
4. Gather it as tightly as possible and tie the thread. Add more stuffing if necessary.
5. Squeeze the pumpkin into a round shape. Use the sewn section as the bottom of the pumpkin.
6. Add eyes, a nose and a mouth cut from black paper and a stem cut from green paper.
7. Cut leaves from different colored construction paper and tape them around the bottom of the pumpkin.

Small Pumpkin Centerpiece

Materials:

Orange crepe paper
Black, green, red, yellow, and orange construction paper
Newspapers
Glue

Method:

1. Cut a piece of orange crepe paper 20″ x 26″.
2. Glue the 20″ ends together to form a tube.
3. Gather and tie one end. Then turn the pumpkin right side out.
4. Stuff it with newspaper.
5. Gather the top and tie it tightly. Push the pumpkin into shape.
6. Cut a piece of green paper and cover the top to form the stem.
7. Cut eyes, a nose and a mouth out of black construction paper and paste them on.
8. Cut leaves out of the other colored construction paper and arrange them around the pumpkin.

Bat Mobile

Materials:

Black construction paper
Two large nails (No. 10)
Tape
Thread
Tissue paper for tracing

Method:

1. Trace the patterns on the next page onto the tissue paper, transfer them to the black paper, and then cut them out.
2. Tape the two wings together along the straight edges. Do not overlap them.
3. Tape a nail to each wing at point A. Have the heads of the nails facing the front of the wings, as shown in the drawing.
4. Tie a thread, for hanging, to the head of one nail and the point of the other.
5. Tape the body along the length of the nails to form the underneath side, or stomach, of the body.
6. Tape the head of the bat to the heads of the nails.
7. The bat may be hung alone or several may be hung together on a clothes hanger.

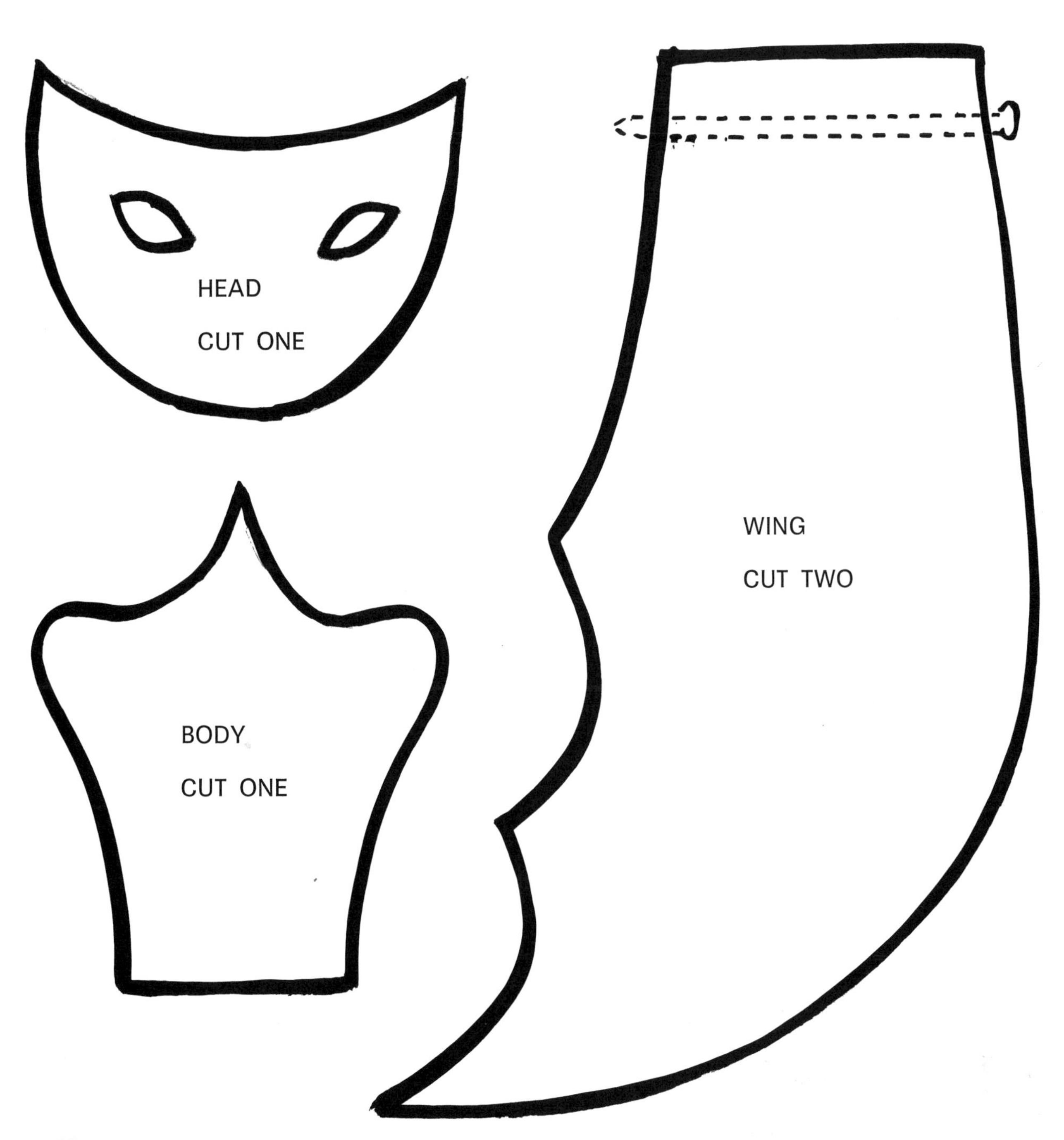
HEAD
CUT ONE
BODY
CUT ONE
WING
CUT TWO

Paper Plate Skeleton

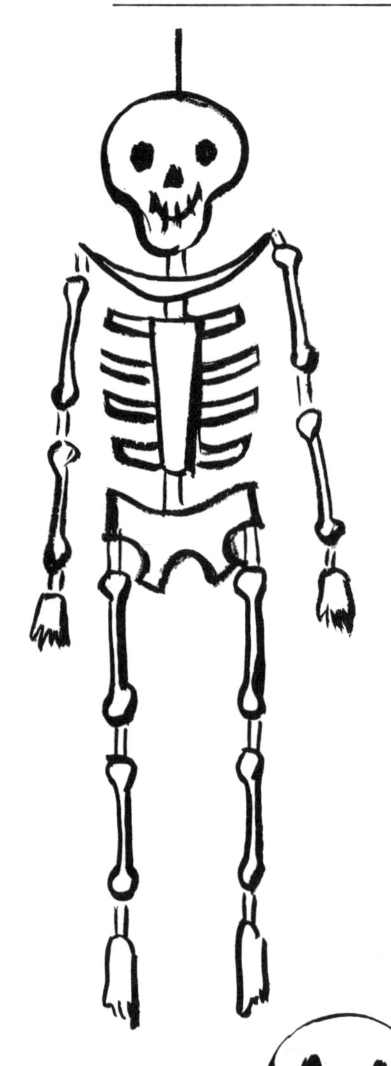

Materials:

22 white paper plates
Glue
String
Pencil

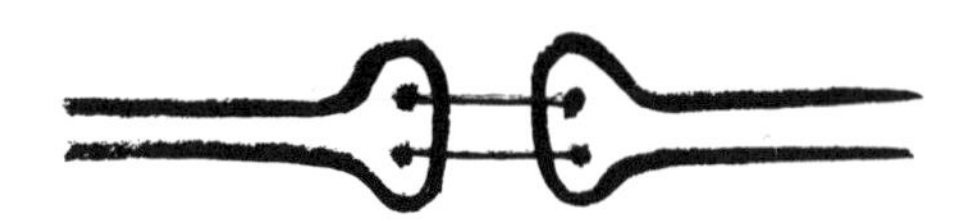

Method:

1. Draw the parts of the skeleton on the paper plates as shown in the diagrams below.
2. Cut out all of the parts, turn them over, and trace them all on paper plates again. (By reversing the parts when tracing, you get *both* pieces to curve outward in opposite directions.)
3. Repeat steps 1 and 2 for the arms, hands, legs (leave out the collar bone), and feet.
4. Glue matching pieces together along the rims. This gives the skeleton a three-dimensional look.
5. When cutting the skull, cut features out of only one plate. Glue a piece of black paper behind the features, between the two head pieces.
6. Staple or glue the upper arms and shoulders together.
7. String together matching joints.

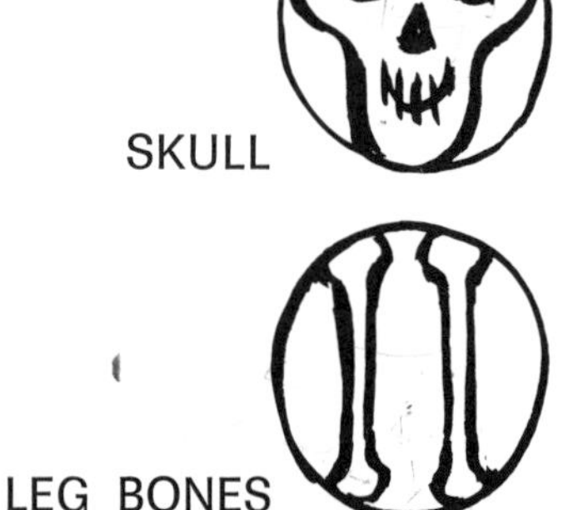

COLLARBONE

ARM BONE

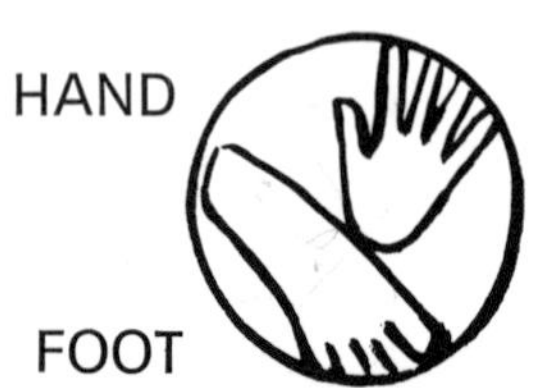

Ghost Mobile

Materials:

Clothes hanger
Newspaper
36″-square piece of white material from an old sheet
Heavy thread or string. Be sure to use a large-eyed needle for this craft project.
Glue
Pieces of felt or a black felt-tip pen

Method:

1. Crumple the newspaper into a ball and tape it around the hook of the clothes hanger to form a head about the size of a baseball.
2. Place the center of the fabric over the head. Gather the material in and tie it in place around the neck with string.
3. Bend the hanger down slightly to look like arms.
4. Draw eyes, a nose and a mouth with a felt-tip pen or cut them out of felt and glue them onto the material.
5. Sew a piece of thread into the top of the head so that the ghost may be suspended from the ceiling.

Skull Noisemaker

Materials:

Two disposable aluminum foil pie plates (same size)
Glue
Gravel or dried beans
Clothespins
Black oil paint (optional)
Felt-tip pens (waterproof type)
String

Method:

1. Draw a skull face on a pie plate with a felt-tip pen. Use the pen to fill in the area around the skull, or paint it with black paint. Allow the paint to dry thoroughly.
2. Put beans or gravel in one of the pie pans.
3. Spread glue all around the rims of the pie plates and press them together. Hold them tight with clothespins and allow the glue to dry.
4. Poke tiny holes through the rims of the plates at the top of the skull and thread string through the hole to form a handle.

Pipe Cleaner Skeleton Mobile

Materials:

7 pipe cleaners
Black thread
Day-glo paint (optional)

Method:

1. Following the drawing on this page, use the pipe cleaners to make a skeleton. Join the pipe cleaners together where indicated by the arrows. Use your imagination to give the ghost different movements.
2. If you wish, you may paint the skeleton in day-glo colors and then allow it to dry.
3. Attach one end of the black thread to the top of the skeleton and the other end to some high place. A chandelier over the dining room table is a very good place. Turn off the lights before your guests enter and allow them to see the glowing skeleton dangling over the table.

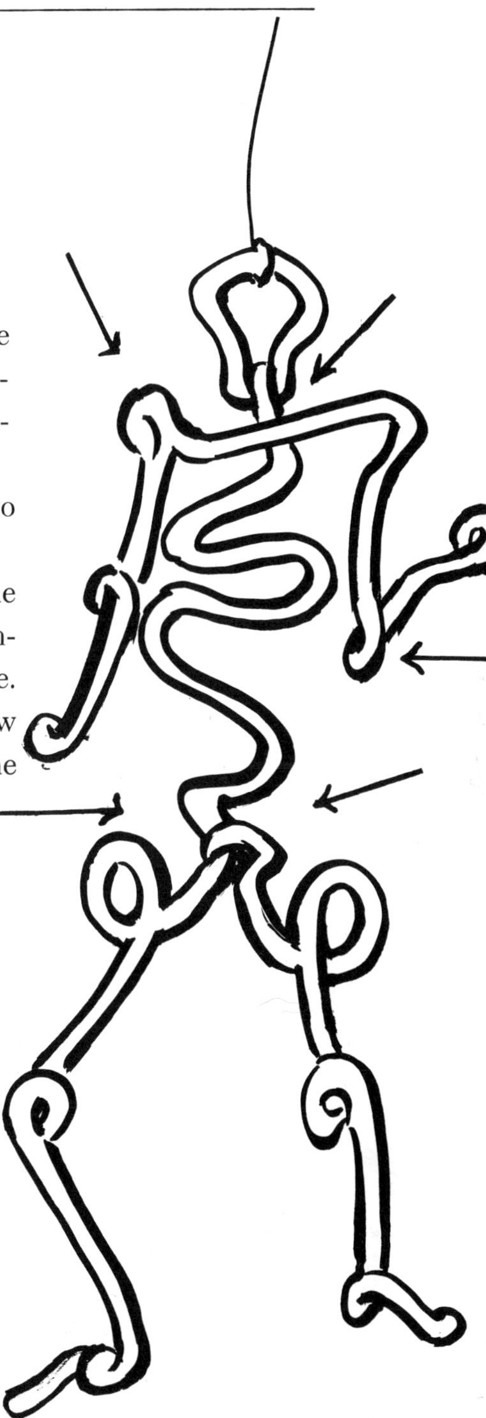

Black Cat Mobile

Materials:

Black and green construction paper
Glue
A saucer, or a lid from a glass jar
Black thread
Tracing paper

Method:

1. Using one of the diagrams on the next page, trace the cat onto the tracing paper. Use the large cat to make a single mobile, or use the smaller pattern to make several cats for a larger mobile. If you are using the large cat pattern, fold a piece of black paper and place the traced pattern on it, with the straight edge of the pattern along the fold. (Do not fold the black paper if you are using the smaller cat pattern.)
2. Cut out the cat's body.
3. Using the saucer as a guide (or the lid if you are making a small cat), draw a large circle on the black paper.
4. Starting at the outside edge of the circle, cut a spiral around the circle, gradually getting closer to the center.
5. Glue the spiral onto the cat's body where its tail should be.
6. Use black paper for the whiskers and green paper for the eyes. Glue these on.
7. Attach a piece of string to the top of cat for hanging it up.

Little Witch Mobile

Materials:

Orange and black construction paper
Black thread
A coat hanger
Black glitter or shiny black paper (optional)
Tissue paper for tracing

Method:

1. Following the patterns on the next page, cut three witch shapes out of black paper and one moon shape out of orange paper.
2. If you want the witches to shine as they move, put some glue on the paper and then sprinkle black glitter on the witches. (Or decorate them with shiny black paper.)
3. Bend the coat hanger as shown on the next page.
4. Sew black thread through the tips of the witches' hats and tie the other ends to the hanger.
5. Sew thread to the moon and tie it to the hanger, too.
6. Use tape, black thread or yarn to attach the hanger to a chandelier, a wall light or something else that is high. Your witches will flash and shine better if they hang in a place where there is a little breeze to move the mobile.

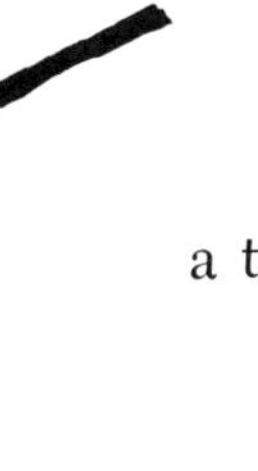

This is an especially effective decoration to use over a table laden with Halloween foods.

Jack-o'-Lantern Mobile

Materials:

Orange, green and black construction paper
Black thread and needle
Scissors
Glue

Directions:

1. Trace the patterns in the book and cut them out.
2. Draw the traced patterns on the colored construction paper as indicated and cut them out.
3. Glue the stalk, mouth and smaller triangles to the corresponding orange part.
4. With a needle make a small hole in the places indicated, and tie the black thread onto the top of each piece.
5. Assemble the mobile as illustrated.

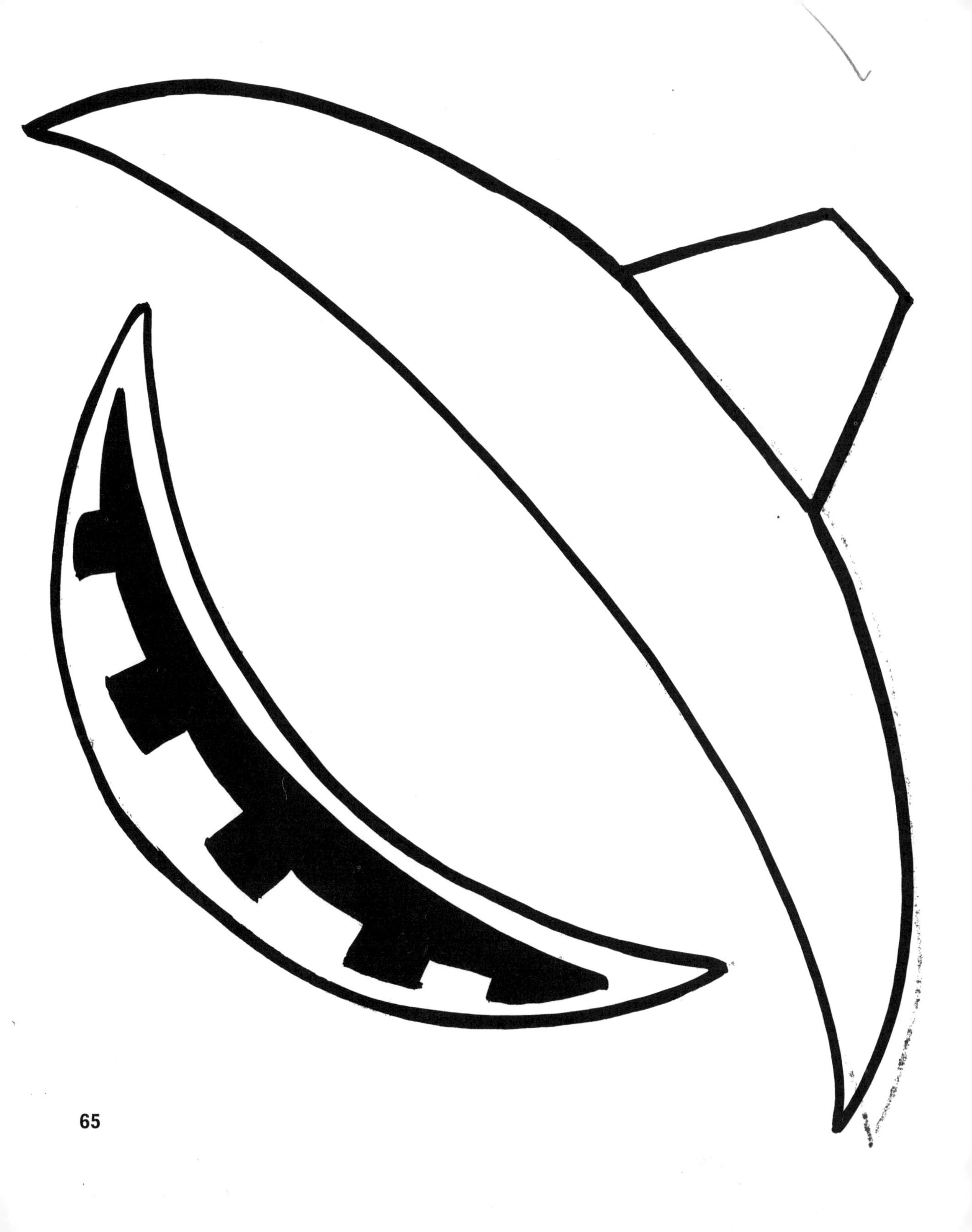

Tin Can Noisemaker

Materials:

An orange juice can with a replaceable plastic cover, or a paper cup

A knife

A dowel rod approximately 10″ or 12″ long and about $1/2$″ in diameter. (A dowel rod is a smooth, round stick.)

Stones or dried beans

Glue

Poster paint or colored construction paper

Method:

1. With the knife, cut an X-shaped opening in the center of the removable lid of the orange juice can. (If you have never used a knife before, ask another person to help you cut the opening.)
2. If you are using a cup, trace the opening of the cup onto a piece of cardboard, and then cut out this round piece.
3. Cut the X-opening in the center of the cardboard circle.
4. Put a few stones inside the can or the cup.
5. Put the dowel rod through the opening of the lid or the cardboard to the point where it will touch the bottom of the can or cup.
6. Put glue on the bottom of the dowel rod and around the top edge of the can. Put the top on the can and

allow the glue to dry. If you are using a paper cup instead, use tape to attach the cardboard circle to the cup.

7. Also apply glue around dowel and X-opening to secure the dowel rod.
8. When the glue has dried, paint the can or wrap colored paper around it and glue on decorations.

Witch and Pumpkin Party Invitations

These directions are for cards which will fit a standard-size envelope (9″ x 4″).

Materials:

Orange, white, and black construction paper
Glue
Colored felt-tip pens
White pencil
Yellow and green paint (or construction paper)
Tissue paper for tracing

Method: For the Witch

1. Cut 8¾″ x 3¾″ rectangles from the orange paper.
2. Trace the witch face on the next page onto white paper. Cut it out. Add features with a felt-tip pen.
3. Trace the pattern of the witch's hat and hair onto black paper, and cut it out. Glue the face onto this piece.
4. Glue the witch head onto an orange rectangle.
5. Write your invitation message in black pen.

Method: For the Pumpkin

1. Trace the pumpkin pattern on the opposite page and transfer it to orange paper.
2. Cut out the pumpkin and glue it down onto a rectangle of black paper.
3. Trace the features and stem and transfer them to yellow and green paper. Cut them out and glue them onto the pumpkin. Or you may want to paint the features and stem with water colors or poster paint.
4. Write the invitation in white pencil.

Party Place Cards

Materials:

Black, orange and white construction paper
Black and white felt-tip pens
White chalk
Glue
Black or white glitter (optional)

Method:

1. Trace the pattern of the card on the next page and transfer it to paper. Use white paper if you are going to use the witch shape, and black paper if you want a ghost on the place card. Double the size of the rectangle to make a full card. Cut it out and fold it over as shown in the illustration below.

2. Trace the witch or ghost shape and transfer it to paper. Use black paper for the witch and white paper for the ghost. Cut out the shape and glue it to the place card.

3. Trace the witch's face and hands and paste them on the witch. The upper part of the hands should be pasted under the sleeves of the witch's dress.

4. Use the black felt-tip pen or white chalk to draw features on the witch and ghost. You may want to add glitter to the witch's dress.

You can vary these place cards by making any design you wish on the card.

Pompon Pets

Materials:

Yarn (1 ounce of knitting worsted)
Felt
A piece of cardboard, 2″ x 4″
Glue

Method: (For the basic pet)

1. Wrap the yarn around a 2″ piece of cardboard 100 times.
2. While the yarn is still on the cardboard, tie it tightly around the center with another piece of yarn, as you see in the drawing. Make sure you catch all the pieces of yarn.
3. Cut the yarn at the opposite end of the cardboard, and remove the cardboard.
4. Hold the tied string and pull the pompon together through your hand so that the cut ends are pulled together but still stick out of your hand. In this way you can see if the ends are even. Trim the yarn until all pieces are the same length.
5. Glue the yarn onto a circle of felt 4½″ in diameter.
6. Features can be made from pieces of felt, which are then glued on.
7. Note: These are very nice party favors which the guests can wear.

OWL

1. Use brown yarn and felt.
2. Cut the 4½″ circle of felt as in the basic directions, but cut two ears at the top, as you see on the owl below.
3. Cut a piece of yellow felt for a nose.
4. For the eyes cut two yellow ovals and two smaller black circles. Glue the circles onto the ovals and then glue the entire eye onto the pompon.

CAT

1. Use black yarn and felt.
2. When cutting the 4½″ felt circle, cut two ears at the top.
3. Cut a triangle of pink felt for a nose.
4. Cut whiskers from black felt.
5. Use yellow for the oval part of the eye and green for the pupil.

Paper Pumpkin Candy Cup

Materials:

Orange and green construction paper
Felt-tip pens
Tape
Stapler or glue

Method:

1. Trace the pattern on the next page and transfer it to orange construction paper. Cut it out.
2. Bend the long strip of paper into a cylinder and fasten the ends together with staples or strong glue. This forms the sides of the cup.
3. Put the cup that you have just formed on the orange construction paper and trace around the outside of the circle for the bottom of the cup.
4. Cut out the circle and attach it to the cup with tape. This cup is particularly bright and attractive when filled with Halloween candies, but any candy will do.
5. Trace a stem onto the green paper and paste it on the pumpkin.

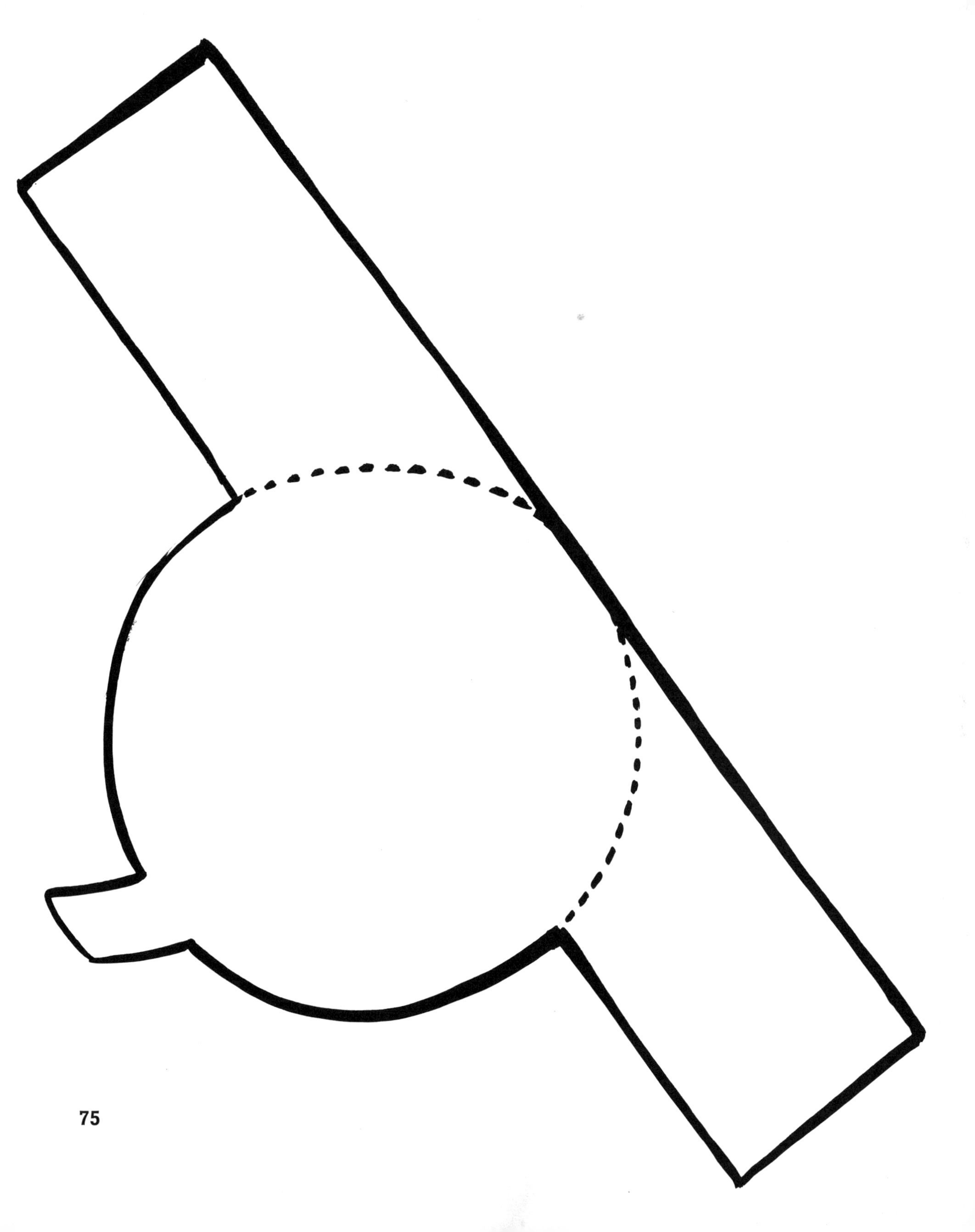

Big Nose Paper Cup Witch

This party craft piece may be used as a small centerpiece, candy cup, puppet or drinking cup. Maybe it is most fun as a drinking cup because of the surprise friends will get when they take off the witch's hat and find it filled with something good to drink.

Materials:

A paper cup with a handle
Black crepe paper
Black and white construction paper
Orange and black felt-tip pens or poster paint
White or flesh-color poster paint
Masking tape

Method:

1. Glue the 2 pieces of the cup's handle together to form a nose.
2. Trace the nose pattern on the next page onto the white construction paper. Cut it out, fold along the dotted line, and tape it over the handle.
3. If the paper cup is decorated, paint it a white or flesh color.
4. Paint or draw eyes and a mouth.
5. Cut a 4½″ x 6″ piece of black crepe paper. Cut the paper to form hair, as you see in the drawing, and glue it to the cup.

6. Follow the directions on page 28 to make a black hat.
7. Cut and glue the hat in place.

PUPPET

Turn the cup upside down this time, and make the witch as described above. Attach a piece of crepe paper around the opening of the cup. This forms the sleeve of the puppet.

CANDY CUP OR DRINKING CUP

Follow all directions for making the witch, but don't glue the hat on. Fill the cup with candy or something to drink and put the hat in place.

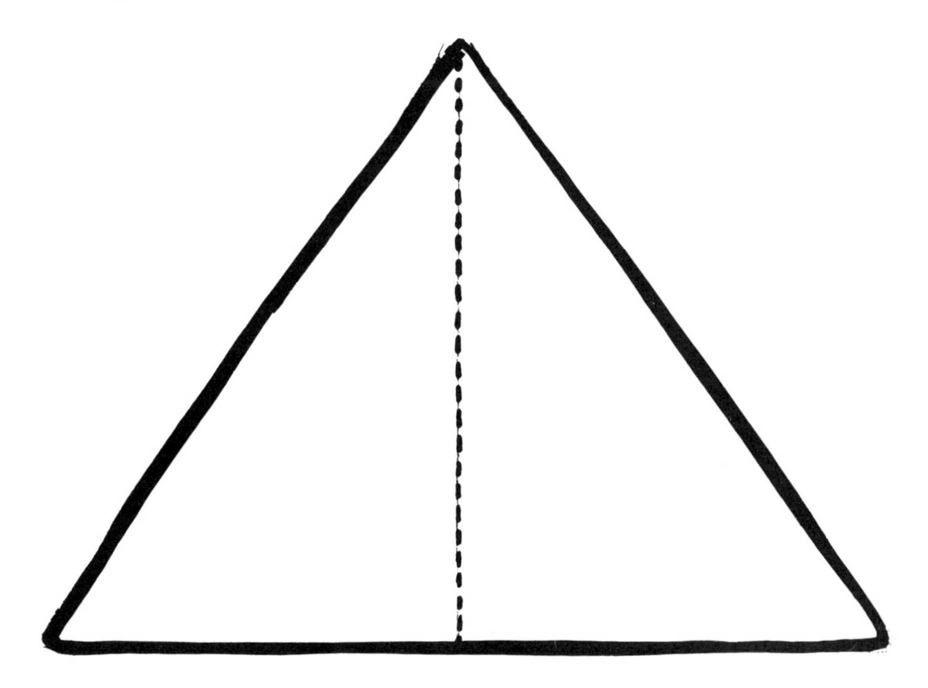

Wise Owl Pin

Materials:

Scraps of black, yellow and brown felt
Glue
Black sequins (optional)
A small safety pin
A felt point pen
Cardboard (optional)

Method:

1. Trace the outline of the owl's body from the pattern on this page.
2. Cut it out. Put the pattern down on brown felt and trace around it with a pen. Cut out the brown felt.
3. Trace the eyes, and cut them out of the yellow felt.
4. Use black felt or sequins for the pupils.
5. Cut a small piece of yellow felt for the nose and paste it on.
6. Sew a safety pin on the back of the brown felt.
7. If you want to make the pin firmer, trace the owl shape onto the cardboard, cut it out and paste it on the back of the felt. Attach the pin with tape to the cardboard.

Black Cat Bookmark

Materials:

Black, green, and white felt
White, and green thread
A white pencil
White thread for whiskers
Wiggle eyes from a craft store (optional)
Cardboard for a heavier bookmark

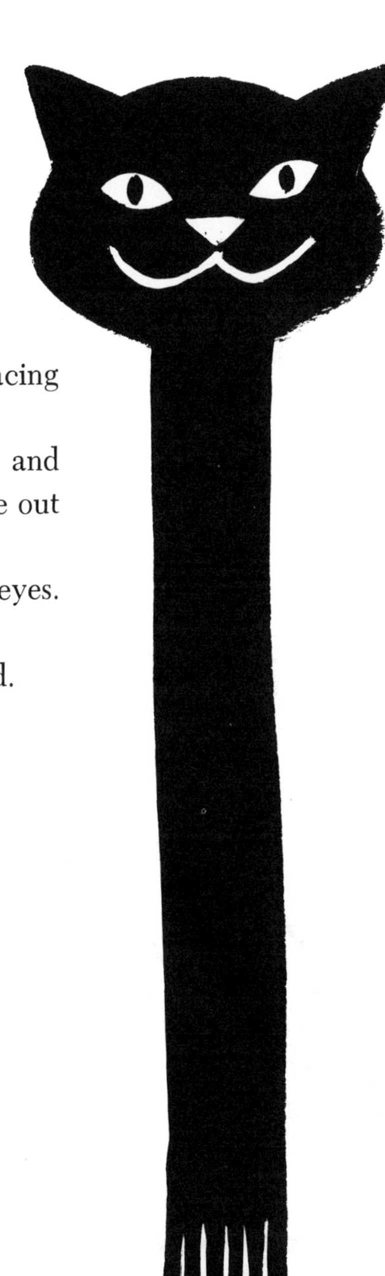

Method:

1. Trace the pattern to the right on a piece of tracing paper. Cut the shape out.
2. Place the traced shape on a piece of black felt and pencil around it with a white pencil. Cut the shape out of the felt.
3. Cut eyes out of green felt. If you wish, add wiggle eyes.
4. Cut a nose and mouth out of white felt.
5. Glue the nose, mouth, and eyes onto the cat head.
6. Cut fringe at the bottom.

Scarecrows and

Jack-o'-Lanterns and Trick-or-Treat Bags

Garden Scarecrow

Materials:

A 5′- or 6′-long stick or post
A 4′ stick for the shoulders
A 3′ stick for the waist
A large paper bag
Old clothes and a hat
Straw (Crumpled newspapers may be used for stuffing.)
Paint, felt-tip pens or crayons
String
Hammer and nails (optional)

Method:

1. Nail or tie the 4′ stick across the 6′ stick about 1′ down from the top. This will serve as the arms and the shoulders. Nail or tie the 3′ stick across the 6′ stick 18″ below the shoulders. This forms the waist.
2. Put an old coat or shirt on the frame and stuff it with straw (or crumpled newspapers), allowing some of the straw to stick out of the sleeves. Tie the ends of the sleeves with string so the stuffing won't fall out.
3. Fill the pants with straw or newspapers. Put them on the frame by putting the frame through one leg. Tie the ends of the legs with string and tie the pants over the waist stick. Some straw should also be left hanging out of the leg openings.

4. Draw eyes, a nose and a mouth on the paper bag and color them.
5. Fill the bag with straw and tie it over the top post of the frame.
6. Use straw for the hair and place a floppy old hat on top of the head. Your scarecrow is now ready to be stuck into the ground to scare either crows or people.

Porch Scarecrow

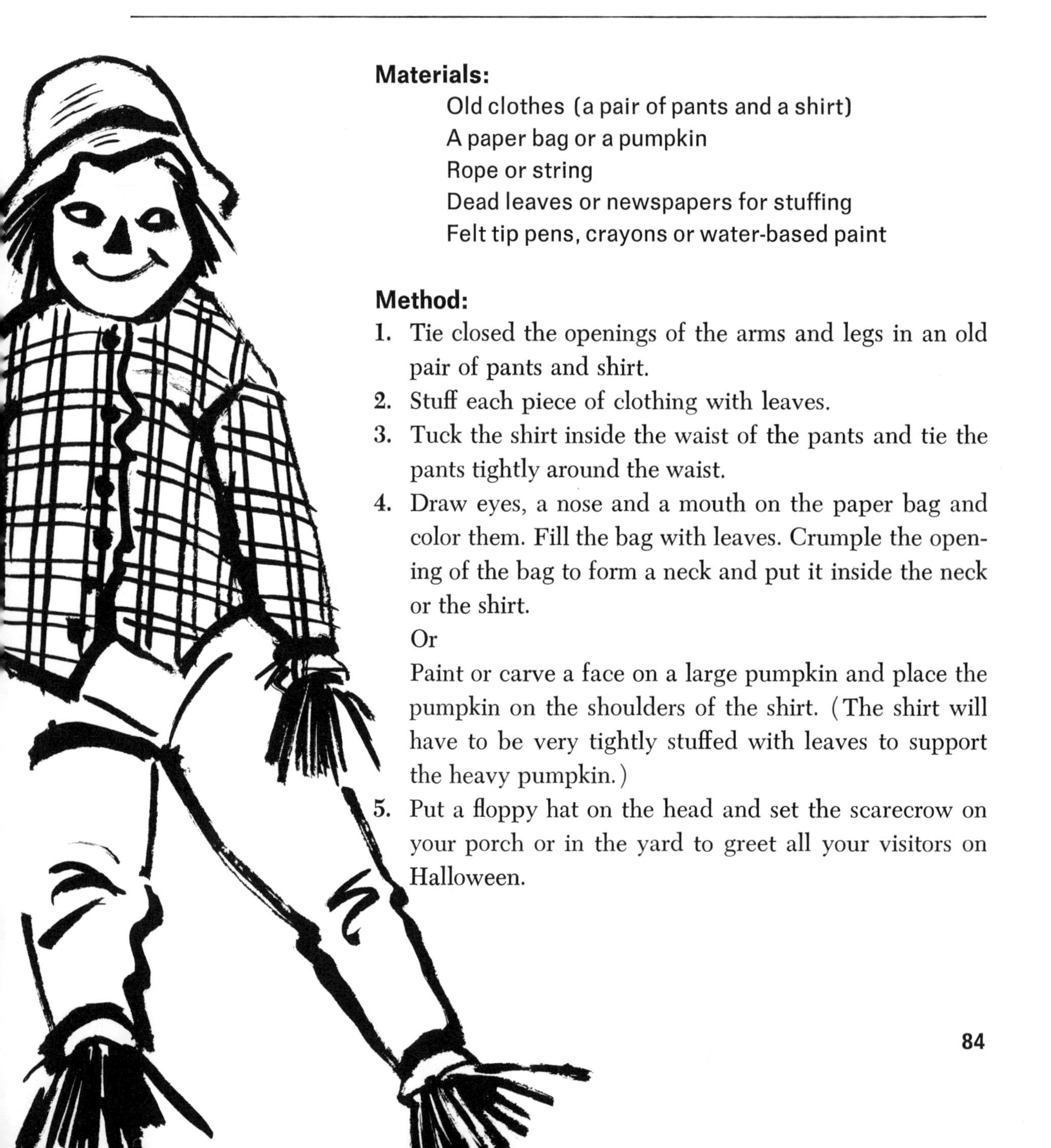

Materials:

Old clothes (a pair of pants and a shirt)
A paper bag or a pumpkin
Rope or string
Dead leaves or newspapers for stuffing
Felt tip pens, crayons or water-based paint

Method:

1. Tie closed the openings of the arms and legs in an old pair of pants and shirt.
2. Stuff each piece of clothing with leaves.
3. Tuck the shirt inside the waist of the pants and tie the pants tightly around the waist.
4. Draw eyes, a nose and a mouth on the paper bag and color them. Fill the bag with leaves. Crumple the opening of the bag to form a neck and put it inside the neck or the shirt.

   Or

   Paint or carve a face on a large pumpkin and place the pumpkin on the shoulders of the shirt. (The shirt will have to be very tightly stuffed with leaves to support the heavy pumpkin.)
5. Put a floppy hat on the head and set the scarecrow on your porch or in the yard to greet all your visitors on Halloween.

Jack-o'-Lanterns

Materials:

1 good-sized pumpkin
1 fat candle
A good cutting knife
Tissue paper (optional)
Witches or other hat (optional)

Method:

1. Cut off the top of the pumpkin.
2. Draw the eyes, mouth and nose carefully with a heavy pencil.
3. Cut out—or have an adult cut out—the shapes with a knife.
4. Scoop out the inside of the pumpkin and throw it away.
5. Hollow out a well in the center of the bottom of the pumpkin.
6. Pour melted paraffin—or candle wax—from the candle into the well.
7. While this wax is still melted, stick the candle in.
8. *Before* you put the candle in you may want to paste colored pieces of tissue paper behind the eyes. Green can look especially nice. Do this *only* if your pumpkin is large enough that the paper won't catch on fire once the candle is lit.
9. Cover the pumpkin with its top. Add a witch's hat or one of your parent's old hats if it is available.

NOTE: If you don't want to cut the pumpkin you can paste colored construction paper on it to make a nose, eyes and mouth.

Trick-or-Treat Bags

Materials:

Grocery store brown bags. (Do not use the largest size because the handle may not be strong enough to carry all the goodies you could collect in a big bag.)
Colored felt-tip pens
Glitter (optional)

Method:

1. Following the pattern below, draw a handle on each side of the top of the bag.
2. Cut the handle out as shown.
3. Staple or glue the two ends of the handle together in the middle.
4. Draw a scary face on either side of the bag with the pens. Add glitter if you wish—especially for the eyes. You may decorate the bags any way you wish.

Now you have a good bag for carrying home all the treats you will be given on Halloween.

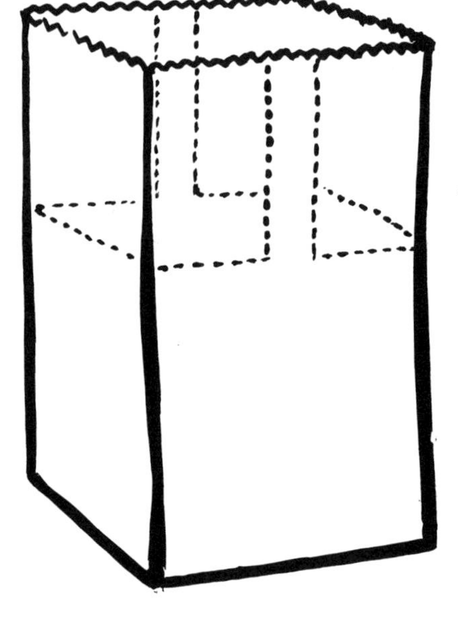

Puppet Theater

Easy Finger Puppets

Materials:

Colored construction paper
Colored tissue paper
Poster paints and felt-tip pens
Glitter (optional)
Yarn (optional)
Glue or tape

Method:

1. Make a cylinder that will fit around your finger by gluing or taping together the ends of a piece of construction paper, as you see in the diagram to the left. Make a cylinder for each puppet you would like to make.
2. Faces can be drawn directly on these cylinders or they can be made separately and pasted on. If you make them separately you can experiment with different faces before you paste them.
3. Ghost, cat or witch shapes like the ones below can be drawn, and then pasted on.
4. Add glitter or yarn for trim if you wish.

Cat Sock Puppets

Materials:

A sock
Thread
Pieces of felt
Buttons
Glue

Method:

1. Put the sock over your hand. Hold your hand so that your palm is down, your fingers extended forward and your thumb extended below the fingers.
2. Tuck the sock in between your fingers and thumb. This forms the mouth. The heel of the sock should be over your knuckles.
3. With a needle and thread sew the corners of the mouth together so that the mouth will stay in place.
4. Glue or sew pieces of felt or buttons on the sock for the eyes, nose and mouth.

NOTE: You can make this kind of puppet into many different animals. Just use your imagination!

Hand Puppets

WITCH, CAT, GHOST AND GOBLIN

Materials:

Colored felt, 2 pieces, 9″ x 12″, for each puppet
Colored yarn
Buttons
Colored thread
Glue

Method:

1. Using the pattern on the next page, cut out of felt two of this basic shape for each puppet.
2. Sew the two pieces together, leaving the bottom open so that your hand can fit in.

   Use the basic shape by itself for a ghost puppet. Out of a separate piece of felt, cut heads for the witch, cat and goblin. Sew these onto the basic shape.

4. Glue or sew features on the faces as shown in the drawings.
5. Add buttons for the eyes.

Wraparound Finger Puppets

Materials:

- Cardboard
- Newspaper
- Masking tape
- Fabrics, 8″ x 8″
- White felt or paper
- Felt-tip pens
- Glue
- Plastic eyes
- String or yarn
- Black construction paper
- Furry material, 3″ x 3½″

Method: (For the basic shape)

1. Using a piece of cardboard 2½″ x 1″, staple together the two short ends to form a small tube that will fit around your finger.
2. Out of newspaper, make a small ball the size of a walnut and tape it to the top of the tube. This forms the inside base for your puppet.
3. Place the tube and ball in the center of a piece of cloth. Gather the cloth around the ball and tube, and tie the cloth with a string just below the ball.
4. Draw features with felt-tip pens or glue pieces of felt to form the eyes, nose and mouth.

GHOST:

1. Use a piece of white material 8″ square. Follow the directions above for the basic shape.
2. Draw eyes and a mouth with magic marker.

WITCH:

1. Use a piece of black material 8″ square.
2. Cut a piece of white felt for the face. Glue it onto the ball section.
3. Draw features with felt-tip pens.
4. Make some hair out of string or yarn.
5. Make a hat out of black construction paper.

MONSTER:

1. Use a piece of furry material 3″ x 3½″.
2. Fold the two 3″ sides together inside out. Sew around three sides, but leave one of the shorter ends open.
3. Turn the material right side out.
4. Place it over the tube and ball.
5. Glue plastic eyes in place or make features out of felt.

Witch and Ghost String Puppets

Materials:

Black, orange, and white paper
Brass paper fasteners
Glue
Black thread
Black felt-tip pen

Method:

1. Trace the patterns on the next page and transfer them to paper. Use black paper for the witch's clothing, white for her hands and the moon and the stars.
2. Cut out these pieces. Paste a white witch's face on the head section. Paste the hands under the sleeves.
3. Paste on the witch's orange hat band, and the moon and stars.
4. Draw the witch's face.
5. Insert the brass fasteners where indicated.
6. Attach pieces of thread (about 2′ long) to the witch where indicated by the arrows. By holding the ends of these you can make the witch move in front of the puppet stage.

Puppet Stage

These instructions are for the construction of a small stage which is meant to be used on a table top. The puppeteer sits or stands behind the table. The same design can be used for a bigger stage to be set on the floor.

STAGE 1

Materials:

Heavy corrugated paper or heavy cardboard
Black tape or plain-colored masking tape
A jar of black poster paint or black enamel paint. (Spray cans of paint can also be used.)

Method:

1. Draw a rectangle 24″ by 15″ on the heavy paper or cardboard.
2. Draw two more rectangles 15″ by 12″ on the same material.

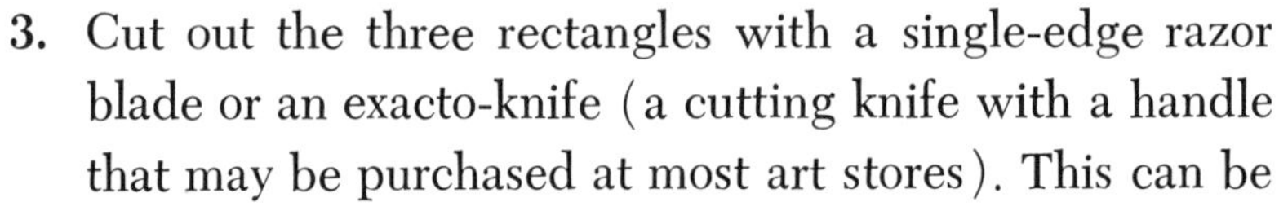

3. Cut out the three rectangles with a single-edge razor blade or an exacto-knife (a cutting knife with a handle that may be purchased at most art stores). This can be

dangerous if you don't know how to use these tools, so it is probably a good idea to ask an adult to do it for you.

4. Tape each of the two smaller rectangles to the larger one along the 15″ sides.
5. Paint the stage with black paint.

STAGE 2

Method:

1. Draw a rectangle 24″ x 24″ on the heavy paper.
2. Following the design on this page, draw another rectangle within the first rectangle, 4″ from either side and 6″ down from the top. Cut it out and throw it away.
3. Draw two more rectangles 24″ x 12″, on separate pieces of paper. Cut all the pieces out yourself or have an adult do it for you.
4. Tape the two smaller rectangles to the larger one, as shown in the diagram.
5. Paint the stage black.

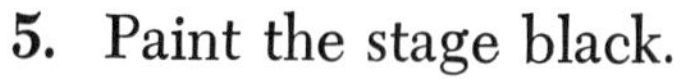

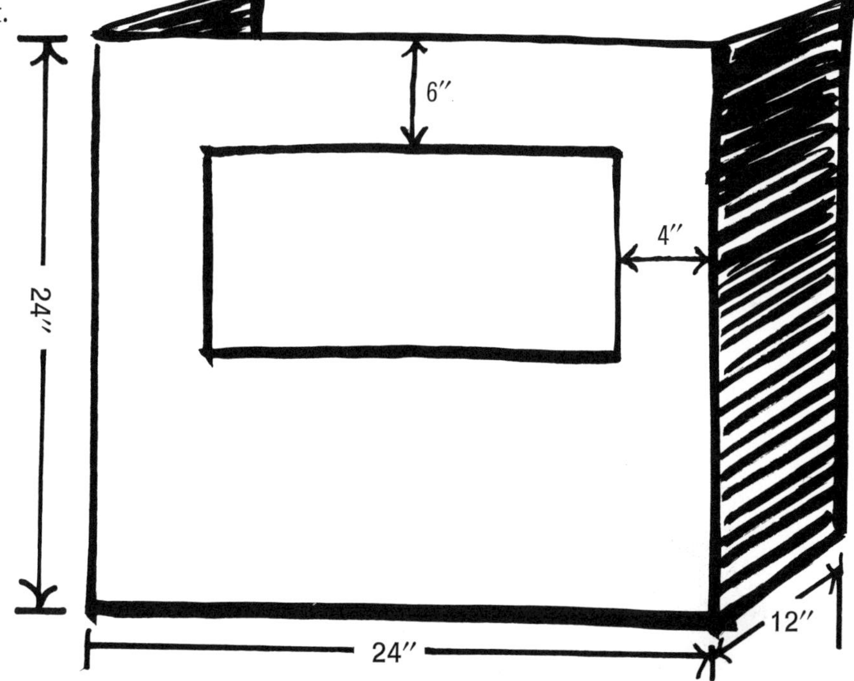

Halloween Party Food

The Wonderful Pumpkin

Long before the Pilgrims stepped off the Mayflower the Indians of the American Northeast were growing pumpkins on the edges of their cornfields. Archaeologists believe that this vegetable was being cultivated here as long ago as 1500 B.C. and have found evidence which shows that it may have existed long before even that distant time.

The pumpkin—known scientifically as *Cucurbita pepo*—was put to good use by the colonists. They ate it, used it as a Halloween decoration, and even found it helpful in the cutting of men's hair.

All males in New Haven, Connecticut, (among other New England towns) were required by law to have their hair cut in a round trim. Usually this was done by fitting a cap over their heads and trimming around it. But sometimes caps were scarce so hollowed-out pumpkins were used instead. This is the origin of the familiar term "pumpkin head."

The pumpkin is still our main Halloween decoration because it makes such an ideal jack-o'-lantern. But pumpkins are much more than that. Their pulp makes delicious pies. Pumpkin bread is equally delicious and tastes more like a cake than a bread. And pumpkin seeds are a nutritious, good-tasting snack. Following are some of the ways to use the pumpkin. Preparing the pulp for cooking is work but is it worth the trouble. This is what you do:

1. Cut the pumpkin in half or ask an adult to do it for you. This can be a dangerous job, and if you have any doubts, do not try it yourself. Remove the stringy stuff. Save the seeds in case you want to make the "Crunchy Pumpkin Seeds" on page 106.
2. Cut the pumpkin into small, 2″ square pieces (or again, have someone do this for you). Put the pieces in a steamer. (You can use a strainer or colander set into a big pot.) The water should come to the bottom of the strainer. Cover the pot. Heat the water and steam the pumpkin for 30 to 40 minutes over boiling water. (Look at the pot from time to time to make sure the water is still there. If it has evaporated, add a little more.)
3. The pumpkin is well cooked when the flesh is soft and the orange skin starts to turn brown and peel. Remove the pumpkin from the water. Allow it to cool and remove the peel.
4. Put the pumpkin through a food mill. This will crush the lumpy parts and make it ready for use. A potato masher can also be used if you do not have a food mill.

NOTE: Be sure that you buy only a *sugar pumpkin* if you intend to cook it. Other types of pumpkins are meant to be used only for decoration.

If you want to simplify the pumpkin recipes in this book, you may use canned pumpkin pie filling instead of fresh pumpkin.

Crispy Pumpkin Pie Crust

Materials:

1 ½ cups flour (unbleached or whole wheat)
½ teaspoon salt
1 tablespoon brown sugar
½ cup vegetable oil
2 tablespoons milk

Method:

1. Preheat the oven to 400°.
2. Sift the flour, salt and brown sugar into a bowl. Mix.
3. In a separate bowl, mix the vegetable oil and milk. Add the flour mixture. Stir with a fork and mix well. The flour should start to stick together to form little balls.
4. Push and pat the dough onto the bottom and sides of a 9″ pie pan.
5. Refrigerate.

Spicy Pumpkin Pie Filling

Materials:

3 eggs
$\frac{1}{2}$ cup molasses
1 $\frac{1}{2}$ cups cooked pumpkin
$\frac{1}{2}$ cup brown sugar
1 $\frac{1}{2}$ teaspoons cinnamon
1 teaspoon mixed spices
(A good mixture is a little nutmeg, ground cloves, ginger and allspice.)
$\frac{1}{2}$ teaspoon salt
1 large can (13 ounces) evaporated milk
1 teaspoon vanilla

Method:

1. Crack two eggs into a big bowl.
2. Separate the yolk from the white of the third egg. Put the yolk in with the other two eggs. Save the white in a separate bowl.
3. Mix all the other ingredients together with the eggs. Stir well.
4. Remove the pie crust from the refrigerator. Brush the crust with the egg white you have set aside. (It keeps the crust from getting soggy.)
5. Pour the pumpkin filling into the crust. Bake at 400° for about 50 to 60 minutes. You will know that the pie is done when you stick a knife into it and the knife comes out clean. Cool the pie before cutting.

Crunchy Pumpkin Seeds

Pumpkin seeds are good for you, so eat them as a snack whenever you are hungry. A single ounce of kernels supplies 160 calories, 8 grams of protein, 3 milligrams of iron and good amounts of vitamin B.

Materials:

As many bowls of pumpkin seeds as you think you and your friends can eat
Vegetable oil
Salt

Method:

1. Wash the seeds.
2. Steam the seeds for about 30 minutes. This softens the outside part so it isn't so tough.
3. Dry the seeds with a paper towel or dish towel. Spread them out on a cookie sheet.
4. Cover the seeds very lightly with vegetable oil.
5. Sprinkle them with salt.
6. Set the oven for 300°. Roast the seeds for about half an hour or until they are crispy and golden brown.

Sweet Pumpkin Bread

Materials:

- 4 eggs
- ½ cup water
- 1 cup vegetable oil
- 1 cup cooked pumpkin
- 1¾ cups molasses
- 1 cup brown sugar
- 3 cups whole-wheat flour
- 1 teaspoon salt
- 1½ teaspoons baking soda
- 2 teaspoons cinnamon
- 1 teaspoon nutmeg
- ½ teaspoon cloves

Method:

1. Break the eggs into a large mixing bowl. Beat well.
2. Add the water, oil, pumpkin, molasses and brown sugar. Beat well.
3. Sift in the flour, salt, soda, cinnamon, nutmeg and cloves.
4. Stir all the ingredients well.
5. Grease two loaf pans. Pour the batter into the pans. Be careful not to fill them more than two-thirds full.
6. Bake for 45 minutes to an hour at 350° F. Let the bread cool in the pans for at least 15 minutes before removing.

Pumpkin Cake

Materials:

3/4 cup honey
1/3 cup butter, softened
1/2 cup plain yogurt
3 beaten eggs
2/3 cup cooked, pureed (finely mashed) pumpkin
1 cup whole wheat flour
3/4 cup white flour
1 teaspoon soda
1 teaspoon salt
1/2 teaspoon cinnamon
1/2 teaspoon nutmeg
1/4 teaspoon mace
1/4 teaspoon cloves
1/4 teaspoon allspice
1 teaspoon ginger

Method:

1. Mix all the ingredients together.
2. Pour into a greased 8″ x 12″ cake pan.
3. Bake for 45 to 50 minutes at 350°F.

NOTE: This is a dump cake. Everything can be mixed together with everything else.

Jack-o'-Lantern Fruit Cup

Materials:

As many good-sized oranges as you have guests
A paring knife or a grapefruit knife
A spoon
Paper towels
Toothpicks
Assortment of fresh fruit
Black felt-tip pens

Method:

1. Wash and dry the oranges. Cut the tops off and set them aside.
2. Scoop out the inside of each orange with the grapefruit or paring knife. Don't throw the orange pulp away; put it into a bowl.
3. Wash and dry the other fruit. Cut it into small pieces and mix it with the oranges.
4. Fill the orange shells with the fruit mixture and cover with the tops of the oranges. Stick them together with the toothpicks.
5. Draw a grinning jack-o'-lantern face on each orange with the pen.

Halloween Carrot Doughnuts

Halloween is the time to make good use of October's rich harvest of fruits and vegetables. These carrot doughnuts can be made a day ahead of your dinner or party and stored in foil or other wrap.

Materials:

3½ cups all-purpose flour, unsifted
4 teaspoons baking powder
2 teaspoons ground cinnamon
1 teaspoon soda
¾ teaspoon each of salt, ground nutmeg and ground cloves
2 tablespoons butter or margarine, softened
1 cup sugar
2 eggs
⅓ cup milk
1 cup finely-shredded or coarsely-grated carrots
1 teaspoon grated orange peel
salad oil for frying
glaze (recipe follows)
about ⅓ cup finely chopped walnuts

Method:

1. Combine 1½ cups of the flour with the baking powder, cinnamon, soda, salt, nutmeg and cloves; set aside.
2. In the large bowl of an electric mixer, beat the butter and sugar together until they are evenly blended. Add the eggs one at a time, beating after each addition until

the mixture is light and fluffy. With the mixer on medium speed, gradually add the flour mixture alternately with the milk, mixing just until it is smooth. Stir in the carrots, orange peel and 1½ cups more of the flour just until it is all blended.

3. Turn the soft dough out on a cloth or heavily floured board and pat or roll it to a ½-inch thickness. Cut the dough with a 3-inch doughnut cutter, dipping it in flour as necessary to prevent sticking.
4. In a deep saucepan heat 2 inches of salad oil to 375° on a deep frying thermometer.* Lower 2 or 3 doughnuts at a time into the oil. As they rise to the surface, turn them over. Cook the doughnuts, turning them until they are browned on both sides, about 3 minutes. Lift them from the oil with a slotted spatula or a two-tined fork. Drain them on paper towels.
5. Set the doughnuts on a rack placed over a baking sheet; spoon 2 teaspoons of glaze over each; sprinkle with walnuts. Makes about 2 dozen.

Glaze

Combine 2 cups unsifted powdered sugar, 3 tablespoons each of orange juice and grated carrots, and ½ teaspoon vanilla. Stir until smooth.

*NOTE: Deep frying can be dangerous. If you have never cooked this way before, be sure to get an adult to help you.

Witch's Brew

Materials:

2 cups orange juice
1 cup lemon juice
5 cups apple cider
1 cup confectioner's sugar

Method:

Mix all the ingredients together and serve chilled. Serves about 8.

Easy Witch's Brew

Materials:

3 cups orange juice
5 cups apple cider

Method:

Mix the ingredients together and serve chilled.

NOTE: Both recipes make one cup per person. Double or triple the recipe if you want to provide your guests with more to drink.

Halloween Candied Apples

Materials:

1 pound vanilla caramels
4 tablespoons hot water
1/8 teaspoon salt
1 cup chopped walnuts
6 medium size apples
6 wooden skewers

Method:

1. Put the caramels, water and salt into a double-boiler. Put hot water into the lower part. Turn the stove on "low" and cook until the caramels have turned into a sauce. Be sure to stir frequently.
2. While the caramels are melting, wash and dry the apples. Remove the stem and stick a wooden skewer into each apple.
3. Put the cupful of nuts into a shallow pan.
4. Remove the caramel sauce from the stove. One by one, take hold of the apples by the skewer and dip them into the hot caramel sauce. Try to cover the whole apple with the sauce. Twirl it around so the sauce coats all of the apple evenly. (If the sauce gets too thick, add a little hot water.)
5. Remove the apple from the sauce.
6. Quickly roll the apple over the chopped nuts.
7. Place the apple with the skewer up on a buttered baking sheet or a piece of waxed paper. Refrigerate until ready to serve.

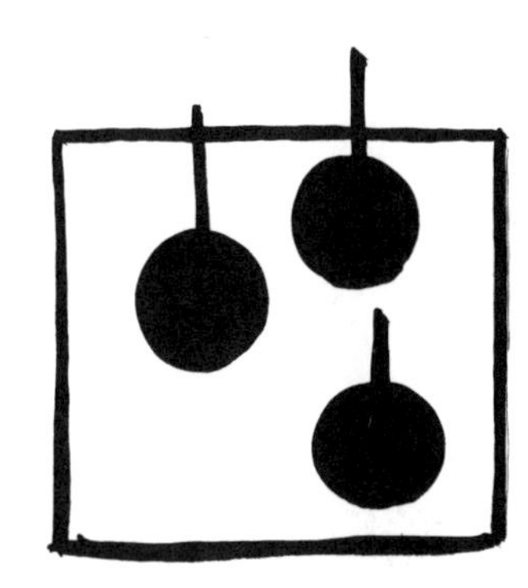

Halloween Carrot Cake

Materials:

- 2 cups flour
- 2 teaspoons baking soda
- 2 teaspoons salt
- 2 teaspoons cinnamon
- 1 ½ cups sugar
- 1 cup cooking oil
- 3 cups grated carrots (uncooked)
- 4 eggs

Method:

1. Mix the dry ingredients.
2. Add the oil and stir well.
3. Add the eggs, one at a time, and mix well.
4. Add the carrots and eggs and mix well. The ingredients will be very moist.
5. Pour the mixture into a 9″ x 13″ baking dish and bake at 350°F for 50-60 minutes.

Halloween Carrot-Fruit Dessert

Materials:

½ cup dates
2 cups grated carrots
¼ cup nuts
½ cup raisins
¼ cup honey
3 tablespoons butter

Method:

1. Remove the pits from the dates.
2. Wash and grate the carrots.
3. Chop the nuts.
4. Grease a 1-quart baking dish.
5. Mix all the ingredients together and spoon into the baking dish. Smooth out with a spatula.
6. Bake at 375°F for 30 minutes. Serves 4.

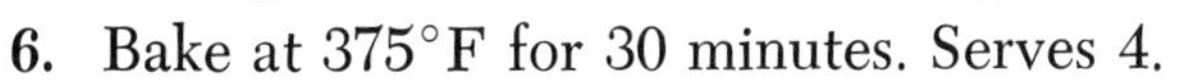

Gingerbread Witches, Ghosts, and Pumpkins

Materials:

- $\frac{1}{3}$ cup soft shortening
- 1 cup brown sugar (packed down)
- 1 $\frac{1}{2}$ cups dark molasses
- $\frac{2}{3}$ cup cold water
- 7 cups sifted flour
- 1 teaspoon salt
- 2 teaspoons soda
- 1 teaspoon allspice
- 1 teaspoon ginger
- 1 teaspoon cinnamon

Method:

1. Set the oven at 350°F.
2. Mix the shortening, sugar and molasses. Stir until smooth. Stir in the water. In a separate bowl mix the flour, salt, soda, allspice, ginger and cinnamon.
3. Combine the two mixtures, and mix them together with floured hands.
4. Chill the dough for an hour. Dust a rolling pin and pastry board with flour. Roll out the dough about $\frac{1}{2}$ inch thick.
5. Cut out witch, ghost or pumpkin shapes.
6. Grease a cookie sheet lightly. Transfer the cookie shapes to the cookie sheet using a pancake turner.

7. Bake the cookies about 15 minutes. When they are slightly cool, remove them from the cookie sheet with a pancake turner.
8. Decorate the witch with dark chocolate icing (recipe on page 118) except for the eyes and mouth, which should be white and orange.
9. Decorate the ghosts with all white frosting. When this has dried, use chocolate for their eyes and mouth.
10. Decorate the pumpkin with orange icing. When this is dry, add a mouth, nose and eyes with chocolate icing.

Carrot Salad

Materials:

4 carrots
1/4 cup raisins
A few drops of lemon juice
1/4 teaspoon honey
lettuce leaves

Method:

1. Scrub the carrots and grate them into a bowl.
2. Add the raisins, lemon juice, and honey.
3. Mix together and place on lettuce leaves.
4. Serve cold. Serves 4-6.

Basic Creamy Frosting

Materials:

1 cup sifted confectioner's sugar
1/4 teaspoon salt
1 teaspoon flavoring (vanilla, almond, etc.)
1 1/2 teaspoons cream or about 1 tablespoon water
Food coloring if you wish

Method:

1. Mix the sugar, salt and flavoring. Add the cream or water.
2. Add a few drops of food coloring if you wish. Mix thoroughly.

NOTE: If you want to make decorative designs with the frosting, you must have a thicker frosting with less liquid. For such a frosting use the above recipe but only 1 tablespoon cream or 2 teaspoons water.

Chocolate Frosting

MATERIALS:

1/2 cup semi-sweet chocolate pieces
1 tablespoon white corn syrup

METHOD:

1. Melt the chocolate in the top part of a double boiler over hot (but not boiling) water.
2. Slowly stir in the corn syrup. Cool before using.

How to Make a Decorating Tube for Frosting

Materials:

1 clean sheet of stiff, strong white paper
Masking tape
1 bottle

Method:

1. Roll the paper into a cone. The small opening should be about ¼″ wide.
2. Use a few pieces of masking tape to make sure that the cone stays in shape.
3. Put the cone into a bottle with the small end down.
4. Fill the cone about ⅔ full of icing.
5. Fold over the top and hold it down as securely as possible.
6. Remove the cone from the bottle. Decorate by forcing the frosting through the small end. This will have the same effect as pressing a tube of toothpaste.
7. If the end it too small for the frosting to come through, cut off a small piece of the cone.

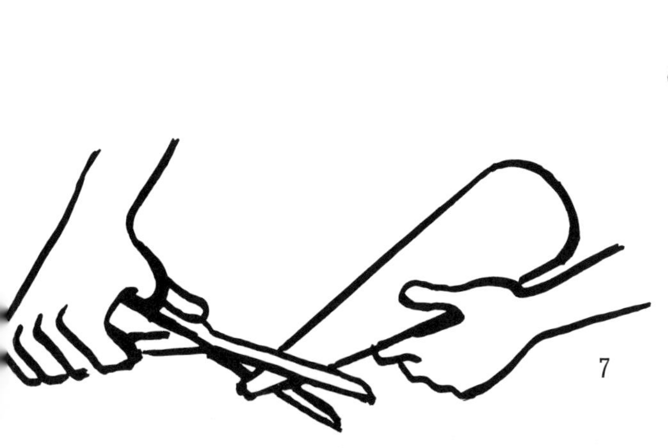

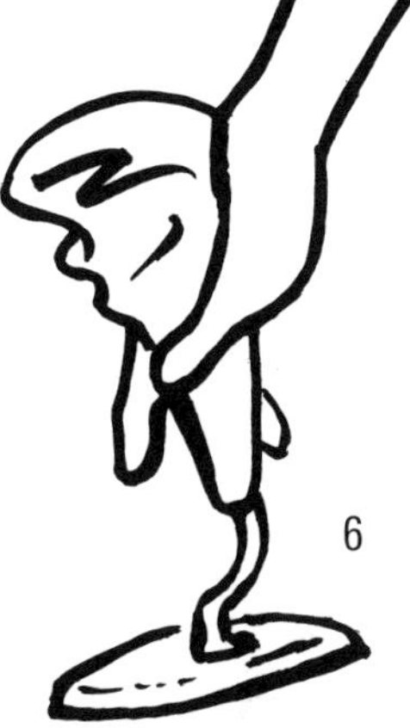

5

Cookie Decorating Tips

Materials To be Used in Decorating Cookies:

Small candies
Seeds
Shredded or flaked coconut
Candied fruit
Dried fruit
Nuts
Raisins and chopped dates
Small marshmallows
Frosting

Remember When You Decorate:

1. Do not frost or decorate cookies until they have cooled.
2. Be certain to put your decorations on the frosting *before* it has hardened.
3. Use a toothpick to scratch a design on the cookie first if you are not completely sure how you want it to look.

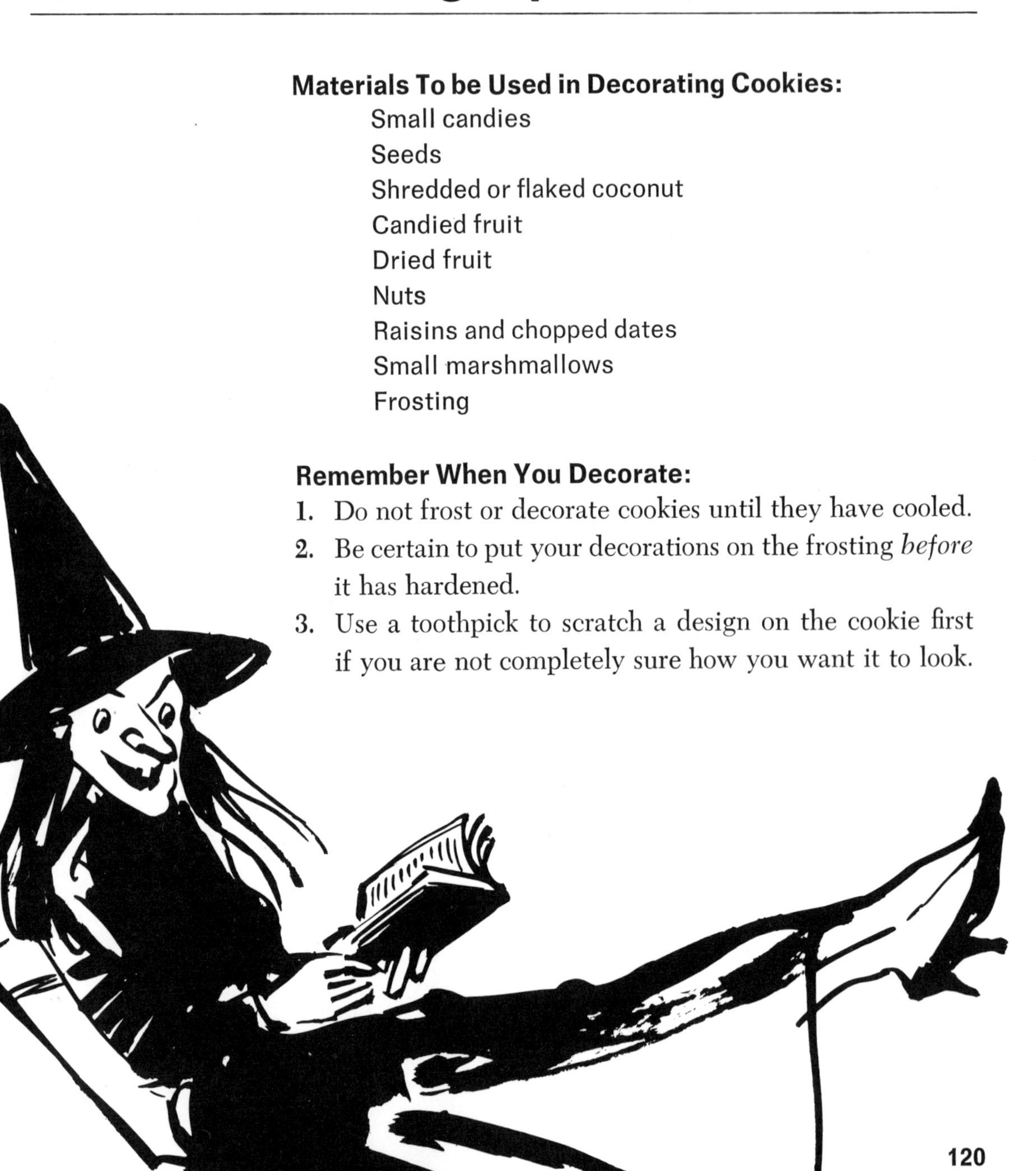